What Happens To My Body and Mind

A Complete Boys' Guide to Growing Up

incl. 10 Ultimate Skin-Care Tips

Puberty Books for Boys Age 9-12

Annabel E. Lewis

ISBN: 9798557156653

Table of Contents

Chapter One:

Introduction

Hand's up if you've spoken about the p-word in school or you've heard people talking about it somewhere else in your life? And no, I'm not talking about 'penis,' although we're going to be talking about that a bit later. I'm talking about puberty.

Puberty is a time of a child's life when they transform from being a kid to an adult. Look at yourself now and compare your body to what your dad's body looks like, or even an older brother. They are bigger, more muscley, and taller than you. Puberty is all about your mind and your body changing into this final adult form.

While many boys find it exciting to be growing up and finally becoming an adult, it's also completely normal to feel a little weird about it all. Your body will feel very different over the coming years, and lots of things are going to change, including how your physical body looks and feels and how you think. You're going to get a lot of interesting thoughts coming into your head, and they can be very confusing and powerful if you don't know what they are.

However, this is exactly what this book is for. Throughout the following chapters, I'm going to talk you through everything you need to know about puberty, so there are no surprises. We're going to go through it all nice and steadily, so there's no need to worry about information overload, and you can easily keep this book and refer back to it at any time over the next few years in case there's anything you want a little refresher on. That's exactly what I've written this book to be, a guide to puberty that's there for you whenever you need it to be.

We're going to talk about everything, including what puberty actually is, what will change in your head and how your body will change, and even what kind of thoughts you're going to have and how to deal with them. Throughout the information, I'll also share some advice on how to look after yourself and make sure you're able to just be your happy self through it all. Then, right at the end, I'll share my top ten skincare tips to help you look your best. As you'll find out, your body will change in some weird ways, so being able to look your best and have great skin is a cool way to feel good about yourself, meaning you'll be confident and happier.

Anyway, we'll get into more of all that stuff later. When you're ready and settled in, let's start with the basics. Let's go.

Chapter Two:

What Actually is Puberty?

If you've asked your parents, teacher, or friends this question already, then chances are you've had some mixed answers, and I get that. Puberty is a word that describes a lot of different ways your body is going to change, so it's more of a wide term. However, it's the best way to describe how your body will go from being a child into an adult. It's time to grow up!

As you get older, your body starts to change in a way that helps you to have children of your own. As a boy turning into a man, your testicles will start to produce semen, and your body will start to become bigger and stronger. In girls, their breasts will start to grow, and their wombs will start to prepare themselves for being able to carry children.

Now, don't worry, just because your body is changing to have children, that doesn't mean you have to have children. Lots of people will wait until they are 25 to 30 to have children if they even choose to have them at all. Just because your body is changing to be ready to have children, that doesn't mean you have to have children right away. It's just a very natural process and part of life that every boy and every girl will go through to get you ready for when you do decide to have them. The average age you can expect these changes to start happening is around 12 years old for boys and around 11 for girls.

However, don't just take this as a fact. Every boy and girl are different and will go through puberty at different times. Some people will start as young as nine, and some people won't see signs of going through puberty until they're 13 or 14, and that's fine. It's important for you to understand that everybody goes through puberty at different times in their life, so if someone starts before you, that's fine, just like it's okay if other boys start after you.

I'll say this once just to get it out of the way for now, but it's so important that you take time to look after your friends and respect other people. Some boys and girls are going to get things like spots on their faces, and other boys might start to smell. Heck, you might even be that guy yourself at some point!

Puberty is outside your control, and it's going to happen to you. As I said before, it's also completely natural, and everyone goes through it, so make sure you're not teasing anyone or being mean. Always think to yourself how you would want to be treated if you were going through the same thing. But guess what, you are, so be nice and treat people how you want to be treated yourself!

Anyway, with that little disclaimer out of the way, and trust me, as someone who's already been through school and college, this is the best advice I can give you if you want to be happy! But I know you've come for the facts, so let's get into it.

The Science Behind Puberty

If you're wondering how all this is happening, allow me to explain in a really easy way. I remember looking up what puberty was online when I started going through it, and it was all complicated explanations and big words that didn't really help, so I'm going to try and break it down for you now.

In your body, you have chemicals known as 'hormones.' These chemicals make things happen in your body, such as turning the food you eat into energy that helps you run around and play and helps your body grow. My body has hormones. Your body has hormones. Your parents' bodies have hormones.

Your dog's body has hormones. All living things have hormones that make them grow and work. It's like your body is full of little potions that have certain buffs.

As we've already spoken about, puberty is the journey your body goes through when it comes to getting your body ready to have children, and when you reach a certain age, your body makes its own hormones that make these changes happen. It's like your body reaches a certain level and goes 'Okay, I need to start changing now,' and makes these potions that start to make your body grow.

In your body, there are two hormones that make this happen. There's the follicle-stimulating hormone and the luteinizing hormone. Don't worry about the complicated names. It's all very science-y, but that's just what they're called. These hormones travel all the way down your body from your brain to your testicles or balls as you may call them, between your legs, and will start helping them get ready to make sperm.

Other hormones are released around the body that will make you start producing hair all over your body and will produce testosterone. Both boys and girls have testosterone, but boys have way more than girls, and it's this chemical that will turn you from a boy into a man, but I'll take more about this later.

The First Signs of Puberty

Already, you're probably asking one simple question, and that's how you can tell whether you're through puberty or not. After all, it's not like you can get a letter through the post saying that it's about to start, and it's not as though you're just going to feel it. I know it sucks, and I wish it was super clear too, but that's just how it is—sad face.

That being said, there are some changes within your body you can look out for that will tell you it's beginning. First, if you look between your legs, you'll see your testicles. A sign you're going through puberty is that these will start to get bigger and bigger. The skin around your testicles will also start to get a bit thinner and redder.

Once you notice these changes happening, you'll know that puberty is starting to take place. It may happen suddenly, and you'll wake up one day and notice a difference, or it may happen slowly over time. Both ways are fine, and you won't really need to look out for them or feel different when it's happening or not happening. Your body will go into puberty when it's ready, so there's no need to put pressure on yourself for it happening. Just relax and let it happen in its own time.

And with that, we come to the end of our first chapter. Hopefully you know everything you wanted to know about puberty and what it is, as well as what you can expect now that it's on its way. Now let's take a moment to look into the real changes your body is going to make over the coming years.

Chapter Three:

How Your Body Changes

Once puberty starts, it will last for a couple of years, usually up until you're around 18, perhaps 20, and then your body doesn't stop really physically growing until you're around 25. However, we've only going to focus on the puberty part of growing; otherwise we'll be here all day, so this chapter is dedicated to talking to you about the changes that will happen up until the age of 18.

As in the last chapter, we spoke about how the first signs of heading in puberty are growing testicles and reddening, thinning skin around your scrotum. These aren't the only changes your body is going to make. These first signs will probably last around a year before other, more significant changes, start to take place.

So there are no surprises, and you know exactly what you can expect to happen, let's dive into them. It's worth noting that not all these changes will happen at the same time and will affect other boys differently. Some people will have more hair growth than others, for example, and that's okay. Everybody is different. That's the beauty of being a human!

But enough talk, let's get into some of the later changes you can expect as you make your way through puberty.

Your Sexual Organs Will Change

Perhaps the biggest change that will happen is the changes that will happen to your genitals, as we've already spoken about briefly. Both your penis and your testicles, which are inside your scrotum, will start to grow and will become darker and redder.

This will happen throughout the four to six years that you go through puberty and may happen all at once, or it may happen in growth spurts. Now, you've probably already heard people talking about penis size, and that bigger is better and that having a small penis means you're less of a man, but this simply isn't the case.

Everybody has a different sized penis, and yes, some people have a penis that is bigger or smaller than others, but that's nothing you need to worry about, especially before the age of 18 when your body is still growing. As you grow up, you may have seen a brother's penis or your father's, and it's a norm in society to turn and compare. As you go through school, you may see pornography, and it's completely natural that you'll try and compare your penis with a guy in the video.

However, comparing your penis size to other people is only going to make you anxious and worried, and it's not worth the pressure, especially when you're growing up and going through puberty because it's going to change size anyway! The best thing to do is wait until you're 18 years old and then start thinking about the size. There are reasons why it will change, such as being cold or swimming, but once you reach this age, you can see if you're worried about the size then. While in puberty, you don't need to think about it.

Your Body Will Start to Grow Hair

A more obvious change that you'll see taking place over the next few years comes with the fact that you'll start having hair grow all over your body. This will start off with very faint hairs over the first few years, but as you get older, these hairs will get darker and more noticeable.

You'll notice this hair first growing around your pubic area, followed by the hair growing under your arms and in your armpits. The hair will start to grow, and over the coming years, it will become thicker, darker, and curlier.

In some cases, you'll have hair growing on your chest and on your stomach, and over time this can grow and connect, meaning you'll have a line of hair growing from the base of your penis all the way to the top of your chest, but this will take years to grow fully. In most cases, it will come up patchy first.

You Will Grow Facial Hair

Towards the end of your puberty journey, you'll start to grow hair on your fair. This will happen around your mouth, on your upper lip, on your chin, and on the sides of your cheeks. Averagely this will start around the age of 16 and will continue throughout your entire life.

However, like every part of puberty, this can happen earlier for some boys, later for others, and not at all for some. When it grows a lot, you may want to think about learning to start shaving. If this is something you're interested in starting, then you can search online for a whole host of tips and techniques to get you started.

You Will Sweat More

Perhaps a not very nice part of going through puberty is that you're naturally going to sweat more, which means you may start to smell. Again, this is a completely natural part of growing up, and every boy will go through in one way or another. What this means is that the hormones in your body are starting to make changes. Sweat is just a natural result of this happening.

You'll find you'll most start sweating under your arms, in your armpits, and between your legs. For most boys, looking after your personal hygiene and cleaning yourself properly is all you'll need to do to keep on top of washing the sweat away, staying clean, and not smelling. To keep yourself smelling nice throughout the day, you may want to start wearing deodorant.

Hygiene is a very important thing for a boy to think about while going through puberty, which is why we're going to cover it in the next chapter, but for now, just note that it's going to happen, and it's something to look out for.

You May Experience Wet Dreams

Ah, so, we get to wet dreams. The chances are you've already heard about these at school or through your friends, and if you haven't, then you will do soon. Wet dreams, also known as nocturnal emissions, are times you'll maybe experience once or twice in your life, perhaps more, where you wake up, and you may feel as though you've wet the bed, but you actually haven't. It's not like fully wetting the bed either. It's more of a little wet spot in your pajamas or on your bedsheets.

Now, when you have a wet dream, this is basically semen coming out of your penis while you sleep, which is completely natural and will happen from time to time. This may happen when you have a sexual dream, or it may not. This will only happen a few times throughout puberty, and then it will stop by around the age of 16.

You may also find that you have erections for absolutely no reason at all. We'll talk about this a bit more later on in another chapter, but just know that they can happen, and they're never to be ashamed of. It happens during puberty, and then, as you start growing up, they'll start to stop happening so randomly!

Your Voice Will Change

Have you ever noticed that old men have much deeper voices than boys do? Listen to your voice compared to your dad's. Try and copy how it sounds out loud, and you'll notice how different it is to yours.

Well, after a few years of puberty when you're around the age of 14, and once you've had a bit of a growth spurt, then your voice is going to start naturally changing to sound just like that! Science wise, this happens because, just like the rest of your body, your voice box and throat will gain mass and become bigger.

However, your voice won't just suddenly switch from one day being a soft voice to a deep one, but it will gradually happen over time. You may find that your voice will sound like it's cracking every now and then, and will go really high pitched and squeaky, and then other times it will go really low and deep, all in the space of a few seconds!

This may seem embarrassing when it happens, but again, don't worry; this is a completely normal thing to happen and will only happen a few times. Just take it on the chin that it happened and let it go. It won't be like that forever.

You May Develop Acne

Acne is a word that refers to spots that you'll find popping up on your face and over your body. Granted, these spots aren't very nice to look at or deal with, which is why if you flick to the end of this book, you'll find some of my best skincare tips to help you deal with them.

These spots can come in many different shapes and sizes and can be blackheads, whiteheads, pimples, or little pus-filled spots known as pustules. Some boys and girls will get lots of acne while they're going through puberty, and some people won't get much at all, or it may keep changing throughout puberty.

If you're worried about your spots or they're making you feel bad about yourself, then don't worry; there are things you can do. You can follow the skin care tips at the back of this book, or you can speak to a doctor who may be able to give you some cream. There are solutions out there you can use.

Fortunately, acne doesn't tend to last forever, and once you reach 16 and above, they'll start to fade away, and you'll rarely have to deal with spots again, apart from the odd one here and there.

You Become Taller and Bigger

Another really obvious change you're going to go through when puberty hits is that you're going to grow so much taller! Boys going through puberty tend to averagely between 7-8cm per year, and you'll get so much more muscular. If you've ever looked at your dad or older people and thought how they get so big and tall, well, puberty is the time when this happens to you!

These growth spurts tend to keep going for two or three years, depending on your genes and your lifestyle, such as your diet, how much sleep and exercise you're getting, etc., and will slow down around the age of 16. That doesn't mean you'll stop growing completely. Most men will stop growing physically around the age of 25, but you can still build muscle by working out and exercising.

During puberty, you may find strange parts of your body start growing, in particular your breasts. Don't worry; this doesn't mean you're growing man-boobs; it's just a natural part of growing up and what an adult man looks like.

Your Mood Will Change

You may have heard stories from your parents or seen on TV that teenagers can be nightmares to deal with, and you may be thinking to yourself, 'hey, I'm not that bad. I'm just living my life. What gives?

For many boys, the hardest part of going through puberty is managing all the new emotions, thoughts, and feelings that you're going to start having. Some days you're going to feel invincible and that nothing in the world can stop you, and other days you're going to feel sad and weak. This happens, and while it can feel really intense at the time, you will get through it.

You may find yourself having mood swings and lacking confidence in yourself or the way you look. You may feel really angry and like you want to go crazy, or you might feel depressed and as though you want to cry. All of these feelings, even if they sound horrible, are natural. I'm going to talk more about how your mind, feelings, and emotions are going to change in more detail in a following chapter, but for now, I just want you to know that it's going to happen.

And with that, we've about covered every change that your body will go through. Now, I know this may seem a lot to take in a deal with, so don't try and deal with it all at once. Just relax and refer back to this chapter whenever something comes up. The more information you have to work with and the more you understand what's going on in your body, the easier and more comfortably you'll be able to get through puberty.

And with that, we're going to start leaving behind the physical things that are happening to your body and start focusing on the bits you can control, such as looking after yourself and making sure you're well and healthy.

Chapter Four:

The Importance of Hygiene

I've spoken a little bit already about hygiene and how, when you go through puberty, your body is going to change and that you're going to need to stay on top of being clean and healthy. You're going to sweat more, which means you're going to produce more body odor. You'll be growing hair which will collect dirt and grime, and your increasing hormones mean your skin will have spots and will become greasier.

I know, I know, this all sounds pretty bad, but there are plenty of things you can do to look after yourself and make sure your hygiene is the best it can be. It just means taking a bit of love and attention in making sure you're doing a few things a day to clean yourself. If you can, you'll feel a lot more confident in yourself, you'll be happier, and so will the people around you!

Now, I know what you're thinking, and I know what it's like to be a boy who's about to be a teenager. Doing things like personal hygiene are easily forgotten and when you're too busy playing or at school at all those good things, then washing your face isn't really a top priority. However, even if you don't keep yourself clean all the time, these are some good tips to remember, and once you know about, which you will after finishing this chapter, then at least they'll pop into your mind every now and then. I will say this, however. It's a good idea to start practicing these hygiene tips as much as you can, so they turn into a habit. If you can do them every day or several times a week, then these are healthy habits that will stick with you for life!

Let's get into them!

Dealing with Oily Hair

More so than perhaps any other time in your life, your hair will get very greasy and oil while you're a teenager going through puberty. This is because your hormones, yes, those horrible little chemicals that cause puberty in the first place, create oil and sweat to come through your skin. It's the same hormones that cause acne.

Every single strand of hair on your head produces sebaceous oil, which is designed by nature to keep your hair oily and waterproof. So it is there for a reason. However, before your body is able to learn the right balance of oils that your hair needs, it overproduces, which creates oily hair which isn't very comfortable. It's this oil that makes your hair go greasy and look so shiny.

I remember in school I was picked on by some girls in my class for always having greasy hair. No matter how much I washed it, it always seemed to be greasy and shiny, and everyone would point it out. It made me feel really bad about myself and really self-conscious, but it wasn't until I got older and realized that every boy goes through this and has greasy hair, so it's really nothing to be ashamed of.

The best way to deal with this oily hair is to wash it every single day, or at least every other day, which means washing one day, leaving it one day, and then washing it again. You can also find plenty of shampoos in supermarkets, local stores, and online that are designed to help you deal with greasy hair.

All you need to do when you are washing it is get some warm water, making sure it's not too hot, and then add a small amount of shampoo into your hand. This doesn't need to be too much; just a little blob will do. Really scrub this shampoo into your hair, making sure you get right down to the skin to ensure you're covering all your hair and not missing any part of it. However, make sure you're not scrubbing too hard that you cause damage. Imagine you're stroking a cat. That's how hard you want to do it.

Once the shampoo has turned into lots of bubbles and covers your hair completely, you can rinse it out, making sure you rinse all of it out properly and leaving none behind. Some boys will use a conditioner on their hair afterward in the same way, but this is entirely up to you. You don't need to use it if you don't want to.

Another thing to remember here is if you're styling your hair using hair gel products. Make sure you pay close attention to the hair products you're using as some can actually make your hair greasier! When you're buying hair gel, just make sure you're looking for grease-free gel.

How to Clean Your Body Hair

When I talk about hair in the last section, I'm only talking about the hair on your head. You don't need to shampoo, condition, and add hair gel products to any other hair on your body. The way to look after the hair that grows all over your body, such as on your face, your chest, under your arms, and around your penis, is by shaving or trimming it, but this isn't essential. Some boys like to shave, and some boys don't, it's completely up to you and your own personal choice. I really recommend trying it both ways, aka, growing your hair and seeing if you like it, and shaving off and then seeing which you prefer.

As you grow older, your tastes are going to change anyway, so you've got that to look forward to. However, if you are choosing that it's time to shave your body hair, then you have a few options to think about.

Firstly, you need to pick how you're going shave. You can use a manual razor that you'll operate by hand. These are usually the cheapest types of razors, and you can buy them pretty much anywhere. If you choose these, then you'll want to use some kind of shaving cream or gel, but I'll talk about that a little more in a bit.

The second option you have is using an electric razor. I personally prefer electric razors because they're designed to be better. They can be expensive (so maybe ask for one for your birthday or Christmas), but they're very good at reaching all those hard to reach places and curving with the shape of your skin. This is an important point to think about.

If you look at where the hair is on your body, let's take your face as an example, you can see that your cheek and chin are not straight lines and have curves. When you're shaving, you need to match these curves. Otherwise, you're going to end up cutting yourself. Don't worry; cutting yourself while shaving doesn't actually hurt. You just might draw a little bit of blood as you take the skin away, and the worst it's going to feel is like a really mild little scrap. The best thing to do when you're learning how to shave is just to take things slow and steady, don't rush, and just learn where all the curves on your body are.

Using shaving cream or gel is something I always recommend when you're starting out because it makes the razor slide over your skin better, meaning you're less likely to cut yourself. It also makes sure your skin isn't rough and dry after you've finished shaving.

The only other point I'll say is that you may want to avoid shaving your pubic area and around your genitals. You can do if you want, and this may seem very appealing when you're a bit older, but the hairs can be very irritating and sore when they're growing back.

Dealing with Sweat and Body Odor

The final and perhaps most important part of hygiene you'll want to think about as a boy going through puberty is making sure you're washing yourself properly. We've spoken a lot about how you're going to sweat a lot more, and yes, unfortunately, this does tend to mean you're going to smell a bit if you don't look after yourself.

As before, these sweat glands that have always existed in your body, and will always exist, simply become overactive. You'll be able to smell these new smells in different places, but specifically on your armpits, around your genitals, and your feet. This does also mean the sweat can come out of your body and will get into your clothes, but we'll talk more about that in a minute.

The very best and easiest way to stop these smells from becoming a problem is to wash regularly. Washing every day is the best way to do this. All you need is warm water like you would have in the bath, shower, or even just rinsing yourself in your bathroom sink and then using a mild soap. Try not to use a soap that's too strong since this can actually harm your skin!

By using such a mild soap, you will wash away all the sweat bacteria that build up, thus removing the smell. Since the sweat can also be absorbed and soaked up your clothes, you'll want to make sure you're wearing fresh clothes as often as possible. Clean clothes, socks, t-shirts, and underwear are all essential for the next few years if you want to beat the possible smell. You can also wear cotton clothes since these are much more effective at soaking and holding in sweat.

If you're producing lots of sweat or you can't seem to get rid of the smell just by washing alone, then you're probably going to want to use some kind of deodorant or antiperspirant. While many people will call these products the same thing, they are actually different.

Deodorant works by covering up the smell which whatever chemical they are made from, whereas antiperspirant stops you from sweating altogether. There are plenty of different types available, including gels, roll-ons, sprays, and even creams, so it's worth shopping around at first and trying different products to see which one works best for you.

Just remember that many brands are designed to make you feel like you need to wear their deodorant product. You've probably seen the adverts on television or online of people wearing the sprays and then being able to get dates and have a better life. This is just marketing, and no teenage boy actually needs to use these sprays. Washing should be fine, but those products are there if you want them.

And with that, we come to the end of the hygiene chapter. Now that you've learned lots about how to look after yourself and your hygiene during your upcoming teenage years, and you're going to smell amazing and be nice and clean and healthy.

While most of what we've spoken about already is about looking after yourself physically and what you can expect to happen, there's one big change we haven't really spoken about properly, and this is the change that refers to the whole point of puberty happening in the first place.

Chapter Five:

How Your Sexuality Will Begin to Change

Sex.

You may or may not have heard about sex, and I'm sorry if you're reading this book with your parents because this is going to go into detail. I'm not going to be talking much about the specifics of sex and how it works because you could write a whole other book on that subject. What I do what to talk to you about is how your sexuality is going to change during your puberty years and what you can expect.

Between the ages of around 12 and 18, you're going to start feeling sexual feelings towards other people. As we spoke about already, the journey of puberty is all about getting your body ready for having children with other human beings, and for this to happen, you need to be thinking about sex.

As you progress through puberty, you're going to start having a lot more sexual thoughts and feeling, and these can be confusing and sometimes overwhelming. You may have already had a crush on a boy or girl at school, or you 'fancy' someone in your class, and that's fine. These are all perfectly natural feelings, but I agree; they are weird feelings you've probably never had before.

Whether you've experienced these feelings already, or you're going to in the near future, I'm dedicating this chapter to sexuality and will be teaching you everything you need to know.

The Basics of Sexuality

While there's a very high chance you're going to be sexually attracted to other people, it's worth saying that it's not guaranteed. You may be really interested in sex before other people are, or you may be uninterested in sex for years to come. Some people are never interested in sex, and that's okay. Everyone is allowed to like and not like whoever they want.

As a teenage boy, you're going to find yourself having attracted feelings to both girls and boys. You may be thinking that's a bit weird, and you only want to have feelings for girls, but your feelings are almost guaranteed to change as you go through puberty. This is what it means to grow up. You're getting to know and understand yourself, and you're going to have experiences that will define the person you are. You don't need to worry about it too much right now. Just know that you're going to have feelings for other people, girls and boys, or you might not, and whatever you like or don't like it completely okay.

To go into it with a little more detail, here are some of the terms for sexual orientations you're going to need to know about.

Heterosexual	These are people who are physically, emotionally, and romantically attracted to members of the opposite sex. This means that girls like boys and boys who like girls. Sometimes, people who fit into this category are known as being 'straight.'
Homosexual	Being homosexual means you're physically, emotionally, and romantically attracted to people who are the same sex as you. This means boys who like boys and girls who like girls. Sometimes, people who fit into this category are known as being 'gay.'
Bisexual	Being bisexual means you are attracted to both the same sex as you and people who are the opposite sex as you. This refers to boys who are attracted to both boys and girls and girls who are attracted to both girls and boys.
Asexual	Being asexual means you're not attracted to anyone, nor very interested in sex at all. Of course, being asexual means you still want to have emotional relationships with other people, but you may not want the physical act of sexual intercourse.

Bearing all these terms in mind, you're probably going to be asking yourself a lot of questions over the next few years. You find yourself asking, 'am I straight?', 'am I gay?" How do I know if I like this person? Does this person like me? Is this love?

Having these thoughts are both exciting and terrifying. I remember being in school and fancying this girl in my English class. I used to speak to her on Facebook after school, and we used to chat about life and her friends, but she was friends with a big group of girls and was always hanging out with them, so I could never bring up the courage to speak with her face to face.

It seems silly now, but I was so happy to speak with her in the evenings and so scared of liking her while we were at school. I had all these feelings that I wanted to be with her and do things with her like hanging out and watching movies and going for walks and things like that, and everything felt really intense whenever I was near her.

She was the first girl I ever 'liked' but we were never together. As I grew up, I began to understand myself and my feelings better. I became more confident in myself and who I was, and I started going on dates and then being in relationships with other girls. I was also in a short relationship with another guy for about two weeks during college, but then I knew that I wasn't gay.

My point is, you're going to have your own experiences, and you're going to be able to figure out who you are over time. You're going to have sexual thoughts about other people, and just because you're having thoughts about boys or thoughts about girls, that doesn't mean you're straight. This will become clear over time, but as you're going through puberty, try to just go with the flow and let it all be free. This way, you'll be open and honest enough with yourself when you do get to find out who you are and what your sexuality is.

Discovering Masturbation

This topic may seem a little out of the ordinary for you, but a massive part of puberty and discovering your sexuality is discovering how you look and understand how your own body works, and part of this is discovering the process of masturbation. As you get older, around the ages of 12 and upwards, you're going to start naturally touching your body, and it's going to feel good, which means you're going to want to do it more, but then thinking about it outside of doing it can feel, well, a little embarrassing.

Don't worry, almost half of all boys at the age of 14 have masturbated at least once in their lives, and even if your friends don't admit it, the chances are they've probably done. Now, I'm not saying that you should go out and talk to everyone about it. It is something you should do when you're alone and in private, but it is important for you to understand what it is and what it means.

So, what actually is masturbation? Let's start with the basics.

Masturbation is the act of touching your penis and releasing any built-up sexual tension you may have. When your penis goes hard, and you have an 'erection,' this is caused by sexual tension, which is all a part of puberty and your body becoming sexually active. There's nothing wrong with this, and it's all perfectly normal.

By touching yourself, by masturbating, you'll find that you release semen out the end, known as ejaculation. Semen is the white liquid that comes out of your penis and doing so is probably going to feel pretty good. This is known as an 'orgasm.' However, you may not ejaculate every single time you masturbate.

It's important to note that despite any rumors you have had heard, masturbation is not going to physically harm you in any way. Sure, if you masturbate incredibly hard or very often, then it can rub the skin and cause irritation, but some of the crazy rumors you may hear are simply not true. Some of these rumors may include things like;

- Going blind

- Becoming ill or being sick

- Not being able to grow taller

- Growing hair or spots on your hands or skin

- Never being able to have sex with someone else

- You will run out of sperm and not be able to ejaculate

- You will never be able to children

- Everything is going to know you did it just by looking at you

None of these statements are true and are never going to happen, so you don't need to worry about it. Masturbation is a very natural part of growing up, although it may not be spoken about in some families.

The important thing to remember is that masturbation is a choice. As you grow up, you're going to hear people talking about it, and others will have mixed opinions. Some people will think it's amazing and some people will find it horrible. The truth is, it doesn't matter what anybody else thinks; it's completely up to you and how you feel. If you want to do it, you can do it, and if you don't, then you don't have to. It's your choice entirely.

You may not think that you want to do it now, and that's okay. If you change your mind in a year, then that's also okay. It's your body, and you can choose to do it if you want. You don't need to feel shame or embarrassed about masturbating because it's nothing to do with anybody else, and nobody else needs to know. You also don't need to feel guilty about it.

You also don't need to worry about catching a sexually transmitted disease (STD) from masturbating because that's impossible, and masturbating doesn't mean you've lost your virginity.

As you grow older, especially since technology like phones and computers are all around us, the chances are you're going to be introduced to pornography. Now, I'm not here to tell you whether you can or can't watch pornography because it's your choice, and the chances are your curiosity will get the better of you, and you'll end up watching it from time to time, but I will say this.

What you see in pornography is not real, and it is conducted by actors who are paid to be in the movies and act, just like people do in the movies you see when you go to the cinema. Pornography is not an accurate example of what sex is like in real life, and the people in the movies are usually modified to look a certain way.

For example, a penis may have had an operation to be much bigger than it was in real life, and female breasts may also be enlarged, meaning everyday people, like the people in your life, will not look the same. Because of these unrealistic differences, you should never compare yourself or the act of sex with another person to what you see in porn because it isn't real.

Also, watching pornography at a young age can lay the foundations for pornography addiction in later life, which means you can quickly become reliant on watching it for any kind of sexual stimulation. While you're perhaps not thinking about having sex with other people right now, these are thoughts that you're going to have over the coming years, so try to keep the two separate in your mind. The sexual experiences you have with other people will be very different from the experiences you see in porn, so always remember that going forward.

What You Need to Know About LGBT

I can't talk about sexuality without talking about LGBT. We live in a time where the opinions of LGBT people are starting to change. In the past, when I was growing up as a teenager, it seemed to be the 'normal' thing that everyone was straight, and anybody who was gay or outside of being straight wasn't normal nor accepted. For people who were gay or transgender, this was very difficult because they had to suppress who they were.

LGBT stands for Lesbian, Gay, Bisexual, and Transgender, and if you fit into any of these groups, you may feel pressured to keep a secret from the people around you out of fear of being bullied, pressured, or teased because you are not like the majority of other people. Fortunately, times are changing, and people are becoming a lot more accepting, meaning if you feel like you're gay, bisexual, or transgender, you can be open and talk to people about it.

However, I would be selective with who you tell. Only tell people you can trust and open up about it slowly. The process of telling people is called 'coming out.' You only want to tell people you can trust because you may not want this information spread around since people who are not so understanding nor accepting may find out and tease you.

Remember, if you're being teased for your sexuality, you need to talk to someone, whether that's a teacher, a parent, or a student counselor. You should never be picked on, nor should you pick on someone else because of their sexuality. It's not fair and not very nice since people should be able to be themselves.

It's worth noting that being LGBT is not a choice. No one knows for sure why people are, and they say it's a mixture of genetics, hormones, psychological factors, and where and how you grow up. Whatever the reason, being LGBT is just part of who you are, and you can accept yourself as being whatever sexual orientation you are.

Learn to Talk About It

Talking about your feelings is hard. I get it. Opening up about how you feel and your sexuality is scary because you're making yourself vulnerable. Someone could say something back, and it could make you feel really bad about yourself. However, you'll be surprised by how open many people are about their feelings once you get over the boundary of talking about it in the first place. It's always hard to do something for the first time.

Just remember, the conversations around sexuality and how individuals are sexually is changing all the time and becoming more accepted by people around the world. The best thing to do is to look inside and see how you feel, and if you understand how you feel and you're sure of it, then that's great and amazing. If you're a little more unsure, then don't be afraid to reach out and talk to someone you trust about it.

As you can tell from this chapter, discovering your sexuality as a man while going through puberty can be a little scary, but don't worry; I'm only talking about the bits that are scary, so you know what to expect. Learning to understand and embrace your sexuality is a very exciting, beautiful, and amazing time because there are so many beautiful relationships ahead of you that you'll get to enjoy!

However, I won't say too much about that because you're going to have the opportunity to explore it yourself over the coming years, so look forward to it! In the meantime, I'm going to explore some more personal changes that are going to you and the way you think.

Chapter Six:

How Your Brain Will Change During Puberty

Ah, how your mind will change as a boy going through puberty. I remember when I got home from school one evening, and my mother told me to do something like wash up or put some clothes away, you know, just some little jobs around the house. I remember being so full of anger, and we shouted at each other for about half an hour. My dad came home from work, and I was sent up to my room for being so angry and shouting at my parents.

The chances are you've been through something like this already or will do at some point soon. It's a well-known fact that teenagers, such as yourself, will rebel against your parents, and it can be extremely stressful for everyone involved. It's a bit of a funny skit when you watch it on comedy movies, but very intense when you're dealing with it in real life.

I remember going up to my bedroom and thinking to myself about how angry I was, and I hated everything and couldn't wait to grow up and move out. As I started to calm down, I started to think more about why I felt like that. My mum asking me to wash up or whatever it was wasn't a big deal, yet it felt like the end of the world.

I wondered why this was the case. Why was I getting so angry over what was really nothing, and why did I feel so emotionally intense all the time? I didn't find out for many years, nor in as much detail as when I started writing this book, that it was all to do with my hormones. The same hormones that are inside you.

Within the pages of this chapter, I'm going to look into how your brain and your mind are going to change throughout puberty. Some stuff you may not understand yet and some stuff you may have properly experienced yourself, but this is all, so you're as prepared as possible for when it finally comes. Let's get into it.

How the Mind Changes During Puberty

When going through any stage of puberty or going through things in life while you're going through puberty, you're going to feel a cocktail of emotions. As you grow up and start learning more about the world and taking an interest in different things, your opinions are going to change, and you'll start having ideas about what you like and don't like. Things you've liked in the past may become boring, and things you never thought you'd like will become interesting.

You're going to feel confused and awkward in certain situations, and you make very quickly become upset and angry with your friends and family, just like I did with my mum in that past conversation. If you find yourself waking up one morning and feeling like you're having the best day and then feeling super sad within the next hour, that's also completely normal for a teenage boy to feel this.

This is caused because the hormones in your body are trying to find their balance. The more of one hormone you feel, the more likely you are to feel a certain way. For example, if your body releases lots of testosterone, you're going to feel really aggressive and angry. Don't worry if you feel like this; it happens to everyone from time to time.

The best thing to do when you're feeling angry is just to take a moment to sit down and breathe. You don't have to meditate or anything like that, but you can just take a moment to yourself to calm down, breathe, and reset. The worst thing to do is to carry on being angry at whatever it is you're angry about because the situation ends up getting much worse than it was at the beginning. However, I get it; people get frustrating at times, so you're probably going to learn this point on your own through your own experiences, also known as the hard way!

However, while this may be natural, if you're sad or angry for over a week, this can be a sign of a mental health problem. Just like LGBT movements, a lot more people are talking about mental health and how much of an impact it has on younger people. And of course, it will. You're going to be introduced to social media and all the complexities of going to school and choosing what you want to be and what job you want to have, and then dealing with everything that's going on with your mind and body as you go through puberty. I get it. It's a lot to deal with, and it can all get very stressful very quickly.

To cut a long story short, if you find yourself angry or sad for a week without feeling any signs of happiness, then you may be anxious or depressed. There's nothing wrong with having this condition, but it is a medical condition you'll want to get sorted out. Speak to your parents, teacher, or student/school counselor to see what solutions are available in your area. I will also make a note of things you can do to look after yourself properly and minimize the risk of depression in the next chapter. The most important thing to remember at this point is that you're allowed to talk to someone you can trust about your feelings. It will help massively.

Thinking About Food

We've spoken a bit already about how puberty is a time of growth, and your body is going to grow in lots of different ways and for many years. This growth requires you to eat a lot of food and drink a lot of liquids, so one big change you're going to experience is how much food and drink you're going to want. And you're going to want a lot. If you've grown up with older brothers who are already going through puberty, then you're perhaps already experienced this happening.

It's important to make sure you're eating as healthily as possible to make sure you're growing as healthily as you can. This means eating food from all the food groups, such as grains, which include pasta, rice, and bread (wholewheat). You also need to eat enough fruit and vegetables throughout the day, as well as a little bit of meat and fish for protein. If you can eat healthy foods, you're going to have so much more energy as you go through the day, and you're going to feel way more alive. The food you eat will also help change whether you're depressed or not. Too much unhealthy food is a quick-fire way to become depressed.

That being said, I'm not a total prude, and I'm not expecting you not to eat unhealthy foods, nor should you think you have to avoid them at all costs. Have pizza. Eat ice cream and sweets. Don't think you have to avoid chocolate. You can have all these things as treats, but don't just eat those foods. Eating junk food and takeaways is fine every now and then, as long as you're eating a balanced diet and you're eating everything your body needs to grow properly.

By unhealthy food, these are foods with lots of fat, sugar, and salt. If you eat foods with lots of calories, this can cause you to put on weight very quickly, and in the time when you're growing faster than you ever will in your entire life, that can get out of hand very quickly.

Dealing with Being Self-Conscious

Perhaps one of the mystery feelings and emotions that many boys won't speak about or even accept until they're older and adults are the feelings of being self-conscious about who they are. It's very common and widely spoken about that girls can feel this way a lot while growing up, going through puberty, and beyond, but not so much boys.

But that doesn't mean that it's not happening.

As your body is changing, as you grow hair and make different smells and look different, there are almost guaranteed to be days where you look in the mirror and don't feel great about how you feel. I remember when I was a teenager, I used to have hair growing between my eyebrows. The hair didn't grow all the way across like a proper unibrow, but there was enough dark hair there for me, and other people, to notice it.

I became really self-conscious of how I looked, so I ended up plucking the hair with my mum's tweezers and eventually shaving it off with a razor. It was very obvious when I did this and messed it up because there would be a chunk of my eyebrow missing in the middle, and they didn't look the same. This just made me even more self-conscious about how I looked.

When I started getting spots and acne, I used to take my mum's foundation out of her make-up bag and put such a tiny amount on to make sure nobody could see my spots. Of course, a girl at school noticed and spread it around the friend group, so that made me feel even more self-conscious because it was basically admitting that I was already self-conscious, and now everyone knew about it!

When you're growing up as a teenage boy, then chances are you're going to feel like this at some point. This is especially since some guys will grow up faster than you, and others will be slower, so everyone is growing at their own pace. The best thing to do is just to remember that it won't last forever and that every boy and girl will go through this in their own way.

If you're being bullied about something, then you need to be able to talk to someone you can trust, be it a friend, parent, or school counselor. However, if someone is just mean, try not to take it to heart nor take it personally. When someone is picking on you because of your spots, the chances are they're going to have them too at some point, so just let it go and be the better person.

Your Relationships are Going to Change

How you see yourself is one thing that's going to change, but even bigger than this is how your relationships with the people around you are going to change. Usually, you'll start to want to hang out with your friends more rather than people in your family, and this is a normal thing to do.

Some parents welcome you spending time with other people and making friends, and some parents are going to be sad because it's a clear sign that you're growing up. From personal experience, the best thing to do is to find a balance where you can hang out with everyone! Spend time with your friends and the people in your life that you're meeting, and make some time with your family, because at the end of the day, they're still your family, and they're still going to be there for you.

It's often the case that you'll feel disconnected from your parents because they won't know what you're going through, but it's more important than ever to speak to them about how you feel. Sure, your parents grew up in a different time, probably before there was the internet and social media, so sure, they're not going to understand completely how you feel, but they have been through puberty themselves and will understand a lot of it. This means you don't have to be afraid of having a conversation with your parents, especially your dad, about what you're going through because he went through the same thing!

It's also worth mentioning that your relationships with your friends will change. Like we said before, you're going to start figuring out what you like and don't like, as are the other people in your life. This means people you are friends with now may not have the same interests as you in the future, and you may grow apart.

It can be sad to see people who are interested in different things and then hanging out with different people, but the important thing to focus on is doing the things that interest you and hanging out with those people. This is how you'll make friends and figure out who you really are as a person.

And with that, we come to the end of this chapter! With all this information, you've learned lots about how your mind is going to change over the coming years, so there should be fewer surprises awaiting you. Of course, your experiences will be different from mine and everyone else's. We all go through our own journey, and you need to be accepting of what happens!

With all this in mind, we nearly come to the end of this book where I'm going to cover the last bits and pieces you need to know about, starting with how to look after yourself properly through all these changes.

Chapter Seven:

How to Look After Yourself Throughout Puberty

Up until this point, we've talked about a lot of things that are going to change in your life over the coming years, and you're probably thinking that this is a lot to take in. I get in, and that's fine. Most of the things we've spoken about will happen without you even realizing, and they'll come a time when you're 18 or older when you look back, and then you'll see it from a new point of view. That's the beauty of hindsight.

However, along the way there are plenty of ways you can look after yourself and make sure you're giving yourself the best chances of being happy and healthy as you go through your journey of puberty, and that's exactly what we're going to be looking at throughout this chapter.

I'm going to cover some of the things we've already spoken about just briefly, just so this list can be complete. Ideally, you can flick back to this chapter at any time when you're worried about something or you're not feeling right, and you'll be able to figure out what you want to do.

Eating Right

An interesting way to look at this point is realizing that everything you eat is the fuel that makes you go. Like fuel goes into a car and then it can run, the food and drink you consume will give you the energy you need to get through the day. So, if you eat lots of junk food, you're going to have junk energy.

I know we've spoken about this already, so I'll be quick. Try to eat as many foods from all the food groups as you can, making sure you have a balanced diet that ticks all the food groups. Limit unhealthy foods, like chocolates, crisps, pizzas, and sweets, to special occasions, as well as watching what you drink.

Too many fizzy drinks will contain a lot of sugar, and this can make you put on weight and may even cause long-term health problems like diabetes if you really overdo it. Try to stick with mainly drinking water. The recommended allowance for water is around two liters a day, but as a rule of thumb, if you're already thirsty, then you're already dehydrated!

If you start putting on weight, which is very normal for boys going through puberty, try to avoid looking into diets. Sure, it's good to make sure you're eating healthy foods and not binging on junk food, but if you're looking into diets which can help you lose weight in two to six weeks or get you a six pack in no time at all, these crash diets are not a very healthy way of doing this, so avoid them if possible.

Exercising Regularly

Exercising regularly goes hand in hand with eating and drinking properly. Exercise is important because it's going to keep you fit and healthy, which means you'll have the energy for your body to grow properly. If you don't exercise, you can put on weight, lose all your energy reserves, and you're not going to feel very fulfilled with your life. Being a couch potato is one of the best ways to become depressed and stressed.

Of course, the easiest way to do some exercise is to join a sports club at school or out of school. It doesn't matter what sport you like, whether you like running, football, basketball, climbing, swimming, or any other sports, doing a sport of any kind is always better than doing no sport at all.

As a growing teenager who's making friends, you'll probably be playing outside, whether you're running around, going down to your local skate park, or kicking a ball around a field. These are all great forms of exercise, and the more you do, the happier you'll be!

Don't worry, however, if you're not a fan of sports and you don't want to join a sports club. I get it, they're not for everyone, but that doesn't mean you just have to sit around at home all day. There are plenty of other exciting and creative ways to exercise.

You could take your dog for a walk, go for a run, play with your friends, or even have a dance party at home or your living room. While it can feel like a struggle to move around and do some exercise, the more exercise you do, the more enjoyable it becomes, so get out there and do something, and then take the time to realize how much better you feel because of it!

The summary of this section; do some exercise, even if that means moving around just a little bit!

Sleeping Properly

Sleep is so important, and I cannot stress it enough. In adults, sleep deprivation, which means to go without sleep for a proper amount of time per night, is the leading cause of depression, anxiety, stress, and unhappiness. You've probably been moaned at already by your parents for sleeping in and being 'lazy' but sleeping a lot as a teenager is actually a pretty natural thing! Sorry parents, but it's true.

Since your body is using so much energy growing and going through puberty and exercising, this means you're going to feel much more tired than you normally do, which means you're going to want to sleep more. However, when you couple this with wanting to stay up later watching TV, playing video games, and hanging out with friends, it's easy to miss out on sleep.

Having one or two late nights isn't the end of the world, and you're going to have a late night at some point, but if you do it too regularly, this can seriously damage your mental health, and you're going to feel super exhausted and sad.

Ideally, you'll want to aim to have between seven and nine hours of sleep per night, but this will vary depending on who you are as a person. I highly recommend taking a week or so of sleeping and going to bed when you feel tired and then waking up without an alarm. However, you're going to want to make sure you time how long you're sleeping for each and every day. This will give you a clear idea of your natural sleeping pattern and how long you need to sleep every night.

So, if you go to bed at nine in the evening and you wake up at seven, and you do this every single night, then you know you need nine hours of sleep. This means if you need to get up for school at eight, you know the latest you're going to want to go to bed is ten o'clock. Don't forget; it's also very common for teenage boys to nap as well, so feel free to put your head down in the middle of the day if you want to, just not while you're at school!

Getting Help If You Need It

It doesn't matter what you're going through as a teenager these days; there is always help available when you need it. You just need to make sure you remind yourself that you're able to get it. You just need to go and get it! That may sound really simple, but trust me, when it comes to getting help about a problem, you may not find it that easy to speak up about it.

If you're going through any kind of problems with your body, you're not sure about something, or something doesn't seem quite right with your body or the way you're feeling, you can always talk to someone you trust. This could be a parent, a teacher, an older brother or sister, a friend's parent, or a school counselor. If you don't feel comfortable talking to any of these people, then there are phone lines and websites out there you can use to talk to someone.

These services will be available depending on where you live. For example, the UK will have UK phone lines, and the US will have their own, but you can quickly find these by Googling what you're looking for and the problem you're dealing with. For example, if you're worried that you might be depressed, then look up a teenage depression helpline for someone you can speak to.

Likewise, if you're worried about a sex or sexuality-related problem, then look for sexual health helplines that will be able to help you. Just because you're going through puberty and it feels like everything is crazy and up in the air, that doesn't mean you have to go through it alone. Speak up and get the help you need if you need it! And if you don't need it, then that's great as well!

Balance Technology and Life

As a teenager in the modern world, you're going through a time that no other human being has been through. This is the age of technology. Smartphones, social media, computers, and tablets all seem like they've been around forever, but as someone writing this book that was alive before the internet, they have not, and it's come with some unique opportunities that have never existed before.

While you can make your own decisions and get used to using technology, as you can be sure that nearly all the other kids around you are going to be using it, if you want to stay healthy and keep your mind in a healthy, happy way, you need to learn how to balance using technology with doing other things in life. It's simply not healthy to sit and scroll down social media and binge YouTube videos for hours every day.

Try to restrict your screen time to around two hours a day, whether that's watching a movie or TV or playing video games and using social media. You can use apps on your device to track how long you're using your device, and then you can see whether or not you're using it too much. I understand that you want to play video games all Saturday long for hours and hours, and that's fine to do every now and then, but you need to have some kind of balance.

By balance, I mean spending time doing other things with your life, whether that's seeing friends, playing board games, exercising, reading, doing a sport or going to a club, gardening, or basically doing anything else on the planet than just looking at a screen.

If you're using social media a lot, studies have shown over and over that this can make you feel anxious and insecure in yourself and leads to lots of stress and even depression. Technology, like most good things in life, is only really good if you can do it every now and then and keep it in moderation.

Looking After Your Wellbeing

If you really want to take things a step further when it comes to looking after your mental health and wellbeing, then you may want to try some of these lifestyle tips. Firstly, you can get into mindfulness meditation, and this may not be the hippy woo-woo practice you've heard about. There are lots of proven studies that show mindfulness meditation is really good for stress and anxiety, as well as keeping you more level-headed as you go through life with regular practice.

By setting aside just ten minutes a day, you can really tune in to how you're feeling and what's going on. When you're going throughout puberty, and your emotions feel like they're all over the place, this can be a really beneficial practice for helping you become grounded and sound of mind.

You may also want to start journaling or keep a diary. While this may sound like something girls do, lots of boys actually journal and keep a diary as well. That doesn't matter whether you write on a computer in a Word document, on a Notes app on your phone, or in a physical paper diary that you write in with a pen or pencil.

What you're doing when you write is jotting down all the thoughts and emotions that are going through your head so you can make sense of them. You might write about things that have happened throughout your day or thoughts you've had, just to get them out of your head. Then you can release them and make sense of them.

For example, you might write something like;

Today I went to school, and someone made fun of me because I had greasy hair.

If that was just going around in your head, you might get upset or angry by it, and thinking about it in this way is only going to make you feel worse. Instead, you can keep writing it down about how you feel, like this;

Today I went to school, and someone made fun of me because I had greasy hair. I got really upset about it at the time, and it made me feel really self-conscious. I've been thinking about it all day. Why have I been thinking about it all day? I had a shower, and now my hair isn't greasy, and I don't really care or like the kid that was talking to me about it. Now I don't feel so angry any more because it really doesn't matter.

Of course, you can write down whatever comes to mind and whatever you want, and this was just an example, but it easily shows how writing something down can help you look at situations in your life from a new point of view, which can also help you to understand yourself.

And with that, we come to the end of our final descriptive chapter! You've basically learned all there is to know about going through puberty in all its glorious ways, including what's going to happen to your mind and body and what you can expect. Hopefully, there will be no hidden surprises.

But, we're not done yet. In the next chapter, I'm going to answer some of the most frequently asked questions teenage boys have when it comes to puberty, hopefully answering any questions you may still have. Then, as promised, I'm going to share my top ten skin care tips.

I've kept this chapter at the back so you can easily find it and flick back to it at any time, so when acne does arrive, you can quickly skip through and find a solution that will work for you, but before we get there, let's jump into your questions!

Chapter Eight:

Frequently Asked Questions You'll Want to Know

If you have any questions that aren't listed below, then don't forget that the internet has a ton of content for you to search up. Just search for any problem, and you should see something helpful coming up on the first page, but don't forget to make sure the information is factual and not lying to you! You want to make sure you're using honest information for honest results!

Why have I not started puberty yet?

Puberty tends to happen between the ages of 9 and 14, so if you're between these ages, then just hold on until you're 15 and then ask this question again if you don't think you've reached puberty yet. However, sometimes the changes that happen to your body will be very slight, and you may not have noticed them at all, so make sure you're keeping an eye open for them!

If you're really worried and don't think you haven't started puberty yet, you can speak to a school counselor, doctor, or healthcare professional who will able to talk you through what's on. Just remember, there's no time limit to when puberty can come on, so even if other people around you are starting, your time will come!

I woke up with a hard penis. What do I do with it?

Nothing, if you don't want to. We spoke about masturbation in our sexuality chapter above, but there's nothing you need to do, and there's nothing wrong with you. You'll probably notice your penis gets hard for no reason at all while you go through puberty. Just give it some time, and it will go away on its own!

When is the best time to start shaving?

There is no best time because you can choose if you want to shave or not! You're probably going to want to learn how to shave first before actually shaving, so talk to an older guy, like your dad or older brother, who can show you how to do it safely first!

How tall am I going to grow?

How tall you grow during your growth spurts will depend massively on your genetics and your lifestyle choices. There's no hard and fast way to find out how tall you're going to grow, so instead, look at your mum and dad. The chances are you're going to be somewhere between their heights.

What are the weird lumps on my testicles?

It's a really good habit to check your testicles for lumps because it can be a sign that you need to go to the doctor, but don't let that worry you. There are some lumps that are supposed to be there! If you gently feel on the back of your testicles, each ball, you'll feel a lump there, which is known as the 'epididymis.' This is where your sperm is stored!

If you do find any lumps in your testicles that are not these two lumps, then make sure you're going to a doctor or healthcare professional to get them checked out!

Is my penis too big/too small?

There is no right or wrong size for a penis to be, which means there is no such thing as being too big or too small! While penises do come in a lot of different shapes and sizes, there's actually not much difference in them. Size really doesn't matter and won't make you any less of a man.

Even girls are taller than me. Is something wrong?

Absolutely not. While you may notice while you're out and about that most adult men are taller than adult women, you may also notice that teenage girls are taller than teenage boys, and this is completely normal. This is because girls will go into puberty a little bit earlier than boys do, so they have their growth spurts quicker. This is why girls are usually taller than boys.

Girls will stop growing around the age of 18, whereas boys can keep growing past this time and quicker, meaning they get taller than most women by the time they're adults. Just remember, everyone is different, and there are always going to be people who are taller than you and people who are shorter.

Your height will never define nor change who you are as a person.

One of my testicles hangs lower than the other; is this normal?

This is very normal. In many boys and men, the right testicle will always hang lower than the left. This is because the blood supply from your heart that goes into your right testicle is different from the one on your left. I won't go into the science of it because you can look it up online for a detailed explanation, but to answer your question, yes, it's completely normal.

What happens if I have a random erection in class? Would someone see it?

If you try to hide an erection you have when you're around other people, the chances are that someone is going to spot you trying to hide it, and that will make it more obvious that you've got one. Instead, try to act as naturally as possible and don't draw attention to yourself. Your erection will feel way more noticeable because it's happening to you, but you'll be surprised by how people won't notice unless you let them notice.

Those are all the questions we have time for folks! We've learned a lot, and I've managed to cover many of the questions you may have had, or maybe not even thought of until you read them! Again, this book is all about getting you as prepared as possible for what is to come, so the more you know, the easier it is to deal with everything!

When do I get my muscles?

A common thing for teenage boys going through puberty to think about is how you look compared to everyone else. Some boys will get really muscley and toned, and others will not, and this can make you feel a bit uncomfortable in yourself, as well as lowering your self-esteem.

All you need to remember is that puberty affects everyone differently, and while some boys and you may look a certain way today, you're not going to look the same in a few months because your body changes that quickly. If you want to get more muscles quickly and you don't want to wait for them, then exercise more by doing push-ups, lifting weights, and going for runs.

Bonus Chapter:

10 Ultimate Skin Care Tips for Boys

As promised earlier in this book, now comes the time for my bonus chapter, which is going to talk you through ten of the best skin tips all teenage boys going through puberty need to know. I've written this section at the back so you can easily flick back whenever you're in need of a tip to help you counter acne, spots, or greasy skin.

You already know what this section is all about, so allow me to jump straight into the tips!

#1 – Start a Skincare Routine

No, not only girls and women have skincare routines, but boys and men have them as well. A skincare routine is simply the habits and things you do every single day to look after your skin. This could be as simple as washing your face twice a day, once in the morning and once at night, or it could be more complicated by using products.

The first very tip you're going to want to think about is starting this routine. Aim as a minimum for washing your face and skin with mild soap and warm water twice a day. You can use a flannel or face scrub to cleanse your skin and doing it at the start and the end of the day is ideal because you're getting rid of the dirt off your face and refreshing your skin's oils.

If you start getting spots or bad acne and want to start using other products, such as face washes or cleansing gels, then you can do so. The most important thing to start off with is making sure you've got a routine that you do every single day. This is the very best way to get the cleanest, healthiest skin.

#2 – Watch Your Diet

One of the fastest ways to get spotty skin that's greasy and shiny is by eating junk food. The more sugar and fat you eat, the greasier your skin will become.

You can literally see this happen over the course of the day. Next time you binge eat junk food, like eating a whole pizza, eating lots of chocolate and sweets, or drinking lots of fizzy drinks, look in the mirror the next day, and you'll see lots more spots than the day before.

As a rule of thumb, try to keep soft drinks and junk food to a minimum and only to have them as a treat. The healthier the food you eat, the clearer your skin will be, and therefore the more confident you'll be in yourself.

#3 – Learn Your Skin Type

How you treat your skin with skincare products and by generally looking after it will depend on what skin type you have. When you know what skin type you have, you'll know exactly how to look after it and how to get the best results. These are the skin type categories you'll fall under;

Normal Skin	Normal skin refers to skin that seems to have a good balance of oils and water and won't have many spots or signs of acne. All you need to do is keep this kind of skin healthy by washing three times per day, preferably with a gentle cleanser.
Oily Skin	If you have oily skin, this means your hormones are in overdrive, and your body is producing lots of them. You'll find your skin has pores and is greasy to touch. You may also find that you have a spot and acne breakout quite often. Stress and anxiety also seem to be an important way that you'll have a breakout.
	To look after your skin and to make sure it's as clear as you can get it, you'll want to wash three times per day with a cleansing product made for greasy skin. However, just make sure you're not scrubbing too hard as to not cause irritation. Also, wash your hair multiple times per week and avoiding touching your face with your hands throughout the day.
Dry Skin	The opposite of oily skin, if you have dry skin, it means you're not producing as much grease as you would normally. You'll notice your skin is dry just by touching it, and you make find your skin becomes flaky if you rub it a little.
	What you want to do is use a mild cleanser to very gently remove the dirt and grime from your face that you pick up throughout the day, and then moisturize your skin with a gentle moisturizer. Ideally, you'll want to avoid fragranced and alcohol-based moisturizer. Avoid washing with really hot water, as this can irritate your skin.
	If you find your skin is getting really dry, soak yourself in a 20-minute warm bath, but make sure you're not using soaps or scrubbing your skin. Just soak up as much water as you can and dry yourself gently when you get out.

#4 – Be Gentle with Yourself

It can be tempting, or maybe even habit, to really scrub your skin hard while you're cleaning yourself and washing your face, but this can be a problem for your skin. If you're scrubbing too hard, this can remove all the grease and oils in your skin that need to naturally be there for your skin to remain healthy. If you're too rough with your skin, you could be taking away what it really needs.

Always be as gently as possible, like you're stroking a pet. If you go too hard, you can even encourage your acne to come on even stronger than before, so avoid this at all costs. Be nice to yourself!

#5 – Protect Your Skin from the Sun

You've already worn sun cream in your life, but you've probably never actually thought about why you should be wearing it. Without getting too much into the science of it, the sun sends light to Earth in the form of UV rays. This actually burns the skin, which is why you get sunburned. Being tan is just a form of being lightly sunburned.

However, burning your skin with UV rays can lead to aged skin, damaged skin, and even skin cancer in really bad cases, so make sure you're wearing sunscreen to protect yourself when you're out in the sun during really hot and bright days.

Also, you may want to try and avoid tanning beds because these can be just as dangerous. Instead, stick to tanning sprays if you really do want to tan because these are a lot better for your skin.

#6 – Avoid Using Toothpaste

You may have heard that putting toothpaste onto a spot that has come up is a great way of making it go away quickly. This is a claim that has circled around groups of teenagers for as long as I can remember, but most of the time, it simply doesn't work and can actually do more harm than good.

Depending on the brand of toothpaste, the chemicals can actually be so intense that it can burn your face and will leave your skin very irritated. If you're allergic to any of the ingredients in toothpaste, then this can make your skin a whole lot worse. The best thing to do is to avoid it completely and only use proper skin care products designed for teenage skin.

#7 – Clean Your Hair

Since your hair is getting greasier as you go through puberty, this can leave a long-lasting impression on your face because the grease can travel down.

Dandruff, or flaky bits of skin that come off the top of your head, can also make acne happen, so you'll need to do your best to keep your head as dandruff-free as possible.

This is quite simply by using anti-dandruff shampoo, which can be picked up in any supermarket or grocery store. Simply shower or bathe like you normally would and put a small blob of anti-dandruff shampoo in your hands. Lather the shampoo up in your hair twice, so it turns into a lot of bubbles, leave it there for five minutes while you wash the rest of your body, and then wash everything out again.

As you go through the day, also try to keep your hair out of your face as much as you possibly can.

#8 – Introducing Products

There will come a point in your skincare routine where you may want to start using products, and there are so many products out there, it's hard to know where to begin. First, start off with identifying what kind of skin type you have, and then you'll know how to treat your skin.

Remember, you don't need to use every single product out there, but only the ones that are actually going to help you and your skin type. I recommend trying a few products over the course of a few months and seeing which brands you get on with and which seem to have the best results. Don't forget you can go online and read other people's experiences to see whether a product is any good or not!

For a decent, all-rounded skincare routine, you're going to want to get a cleansing product, a toner, and probably some kind of acne gel, medicated if possible.

#9 – Get Professional Help

If you find your skin is really bad and you're getting lots of spots, it's flaking, or you're just feeling really bad in yourself because you're not looking the way you want and it's making you really unhappy, you can always go and visit a dermatologist, which is a fancy word for a doctor who's really good at working with skin.

You should only go and visit one of these doctors if your acne is really bad, and it's affecting how you live your life, such as if it's really painful or severe. After your meeting with the doctor, they'll give some medication, such as a cream or gel, which can help make the acne go away as quickly as possible.

You should also go and see a doctor if your acne is really bad because they can help you reduce any potential scaring the acne may leave on your face.

#10 – Clean Your Hands Regularly

Finally, the most important point to remember is to wash your hands regularly, and I'm talking about pretty much any time you get the opportunity too! Throughout the day, you're going to go around and touch so many different things and pick up so much dirt, bacteria, and grime, and then without even thinking, you'll end up touching your face and putting all that dirt onto your face!

Basically, you're going to want to avoid touching your face as much as you can help it and remember to (don't worry, a lot of it you'll do without even thinking about doing it) or washing your hands before you touch your face.

Hand in hand with this point, also make sure you're cleaning your phone and wiping down your tablet before and after using it, and change things like your pillowcases that can put more unwanted dirt and grime onto your face.

Final Thoughts

And we've reached the end of our journey, and now it's time for you to start yours! I hope you've enjoyed reading this book and learning all there is to know about going through puberty and what's going to be happening to you throughout the coming years. I know that some of it can sound scary and confusing, and some things in this book you might not understand yet but trust me when I say it will all come in time.

As you grow up, you'll become more and more aware of your body and everything we've been speaking about, and you'll be able to understand it all from your own perspective. It's not as scary or as overwhelming as it may seem here, and a lot of changes will happen to you without you even noticing! The best advice I can give you is to embrace all the changes that are happening to you, take them as being who you are, and enjoy growing up! You've got so many bright and beautiful years ahead of you, and you're going to look back on this time when you're older with a smile because it's going to be so much fun!

As my final point, if you did enjoy reading this book, and you got a lot out of it, I would love to hear your feedback by leaving me a positive online review. I do read all the comments back because I adore hearing how I might have helped you, and it inspires me to keep writing and keeping making more books, so let me know, and I can't wait to hear from you!

That's all from me for now, so don't forget you can refer back to this book at any time if you forgot something or want to know more, and there's an entire internet out there which can answer any new questions you may have! All the best on your journey and enjoy life!

Disclaimer

This book contains opinions and ideas of the author and is meant to teach the reader informative and helpful knowledge while due care should be taken by the user in the application of the information provided. The instructions and strategies are possibly not right for every reader and there is no guarantee that they work for everyone. Using this book and implementing the information/recipes therein contained is explicitly your own responsibility and risk. This work with all its contents, does not guarantee correctness, completion, quality or correctness of the provided information. Misinformation or misprints cannot be completely eliminated.

Printed in Great Britain
by Amazon

82110109R00050

The Making of
Landscape Photographs

Charlie Waite

The Making of Landscape Photographs

All the photographs in
this book are dedicated
to my dearest friend David.

Acknowledgements
My thanks go to everyone at Toucan, particularly
Robert Sackville West, who first suggested the idea
for this book, John Meek who designed it,
Jane MacAndrew who edited it and,
above all, Adam Nicolson who has been with
me every step of the way.

First published in Great Britain in 1992
by Collins & Brown Limited
Mercury House
195 Knightsbridge
London SW7 1RE

British Library Cataloguing-in-Publication Data:
A catalogue record for this book
is available from the British Library.

ISBN 1 85585 069 9 (hardback)
ISBN 1 85585 125 3 (paperback)

Edited and designed by Toucan Books Limited, London

Printed in Italy by New Interlitho SpA, Milan

Contents

Introduction:
A Frame of Mind

I T IS NOT always easy to talk or even think about something which you do naturally and instinctively. I have been taking photographs of the landscape almost continuously now for about fifteen years and, rather less often, for ten or more years before that. What I have set out to do in this book is to explore the way some of my favourite photographs were taken – why they work, if they do, how with hindsight I might have improved them, what I learnt to avoid, how I was led many times towards the same certain subjects. Precisely because so much of this was intuitive at the time – the framing of pictures is scarcely a conscious act for me – the writing of the book has been a process of discovery, bringing into consciousness many things which until then had been lurking in the unconscious part of my mind. I only hope that sharing the experience will be of some help to other photographers.

This is not a book about photographic technique. It is, at least to begin with, about an attitude of mind, about seeing what is there in front of you. Later on in the book, there will be chapters about the very specific and detailed ways of handling cameras, lenses, films and filters. But that can wait for a moment. It is important to realise before anything else that all the technology in the world will not matter and all the skill you could possibly muster will not help you move one inch towards a good photograph, if your mind and attitude to the landscape itself is not in the right shape. That is why this Introduction is called *A Frame of Mind*. Your brain and eye are the most important pieces of equipment that you have.

I do not believe that a good photograph can be made without recognising that the landscape will always be more important than either you or the photograph you plan to make of it. Of course it has to be helped and supported by all the techniques of photography, but, when taking a photograph I know to be good, the sensation I always have is a modest one. It is an inner *ah*, the knowledge that something is right. When this understanding is there, something strange happens to me. The heart beat slows down, the whole metabolism seems to come down towards the rate of the landscape itself and the mind, almost as if coated with an emulsion itself, starts to soak up the meaning of the place. There is nothing casual about it. It is not a snatch. Understanding grows as you allow the landscape to come into you. Passivity, not acquisition, is the key to this. A good photograph is a received photograph, an exchange between you and the landscape, in which –

Buttermere, Cumbria

however unlikely this might seem – there is a form of dialogue between the two of you. It is simply courtesy to allow the landscape to speak.

This picture in the English Lake District (above) seems to represent that sort of moment for me. The transmission of the landscape into the photograph is especially pure and uncorrupted. I have not quarried the place, but allowed it to have its say. The picture is not there to make a point. It is simply a recognition, as I see it, of something that is beautiful.

You might ask yourself why anyone should take photographs of the landscape. Perhaps this is too simple a question. The landscape is so obviously a beautiful and alluring thing that even from the earliest days of photography, when it still seemed magical that every detail of a scene could be recorded exactly as it was at a particular moment, people have gone out into the fields and woods to take pictures of them.

But if I had to try to put into words the instinctive feelings I have about landscape, I would say that one of the reasons it draws me – and continues to draw me morning after morning, season after season – is that landscape is something that endures. This is not a temporary thing. I think of those 4,500 million years, the age of the earth. I hold them, as far as one can, in my mind, and the sensation I have is that I am a passenger on the surface of something immeasurably more substantial. And this has a strange effect. I am never particularly worried or disturbed by the presence of a new quarry here or a new road there. In the end, in the sort of time-perspective on which the earth itself works, that will not make the slightest difference. In this reservoir near Pamplona (below) in the north of Spain

East of Pamplona, Navarra, Spain

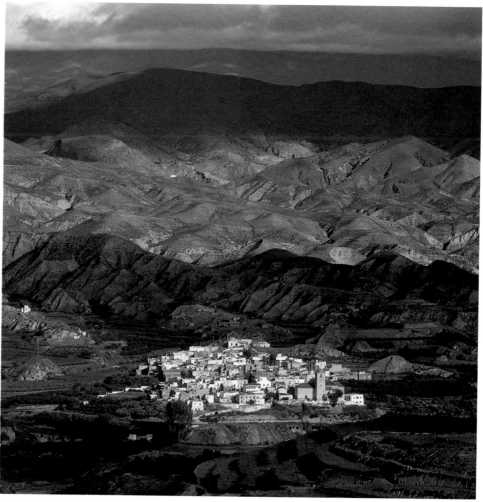

North west of Almería, Sierra Nevada, Spain

or this village in the Sierra Nevada (above) the changes that people have made to the landscape have added to it. And in this way the landscape is a sort of visual memory bank. It is an account of what people and the weather and plants and animals have done there, year after year, layer on layer, slowly accumulating the complex and nuanced patina of meaning which is, I think, what we respond to in the landscape.

The years that I have spent making photographs of the landscape have been a continuous exploration of this extraordinary and resonant surface. Often I have stood for a moment away from the details of camera and tripod and lenses and film, and seen suddenly and again – this is something so important but so easily taken for granted that you need to remind yourself of it as often as you can – that the position we have on earth is, in its way, enormously privileged. The landscape is the thinnest of living veins in marble, squeezed between the giant masses of rock below and sky above. It is where the fluid and mobile element of the atmosphere meets the solidity of earth. That meeting of those opposites is the great drama of the landscape. And of course the catalyst for it all, the one thing that a

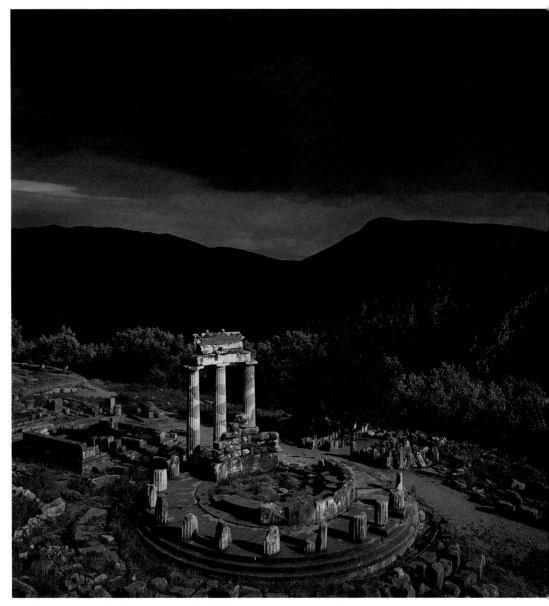

Temple of Athena Pronaia, Delphi, Greece

photographer must know, must learn to understand, must come perhaps, in the end, to love, is light.

Perhaps it is like a love affair. Sometimes the landscape meets you quite willingly, sometimes it is a question of assiduous wooing. There are pleasures in both, but in my experience, the less the image is manipulated, the more perfect the experience for the photographer. Of course there are different grades of manipulation, but if I look at my pictures I will always see them either as pictures which I have had to work for, which are *worked* images in fact, and those which have fallen straight into my lap. I love them both but in a very different way. If it is possible to look at a picture and say 'Yes, I have made that, I have used everything in my power to make something that is pleasing,' then of course there is great satisfaction in that.

The Temple of Athena Pronaia at Delphi (left) is a worked image, one which I can never look at without remembering how I made it. I went back and back to Delphi at different times of day and in different weathers. I felt there was something in this ancient and sacred place which needed to emerge in a photograph of it. And in making the photograph I used all the necessary technical skills – slightly underexposing, darkening the sky with a graduated filter and warming it up with a colour correction filter. I wanted nothing to distract from the form of the temple. I had to wait until there was no light on the hills in the background, I wanted light that was both dramatic and warm – and so on. But I do not here want to go into all the detailed considerations that run through one's mind when faced with something like the temple of Athena Pronaia. The point is this. *The landscape deserved nothing less.* It was right to make it look as it does here, a bright stone laid on a velvet cloth, a thing made holy by the light falling on it and by the shadow enshrining it. It was a question of making an inner and hidden meaning clear.

But there is another sort of picture, one I can look at and see not the picture itself but straight through it to the place I remember. And that experience is one of the sustaining miracles of photography. This picture of a scene in the Alps (below)

Chamechaude, Isère, France

Near Cazorla, Andalucia, Spain

was there as you now see it, perfect and ready. All I had to do was stand in front of it and drink it in.

But don't make the mistake of thinking that photography will always be a relaxed process. The photographer who always sees himself as calm and sedate, as nothing but a slow absorber of the meaning of a place, will more often than not miss the meaning which the place is trying to offer him. Rush to get it if you have to, moving as quickly as nature often does. The quick movement, the sudden noticing of something perfect but passing in its perfection – that too must be part of the photographer's vocabulary, which goes far beyond the boxes of lenses and filters. It is a quality of mind. The shutter in the camera will move in tiny fractions of a second. You must not lag behind.

The difference on the previous page between the photographs at Delphi and in the Alps – between a made photograph and a photograph which made itself – has its equivalent in time. The thorn tree lit like a burning bush (above) lasted scarcely any longer than the second it took to expose the film. Arriving at it in the heart of Spain, seeing it from the top of the hill as the sun was dropping down, I had to race to catch the tree before the light had gone. And it is that instantaneous, disappearing nature of the beautiful moment that of course makes it all the more precious. To capture that is something that only photography can do and it is above all – even speaking technically and chemically – a response to what is there in front of you. The light is going, its beauty is there for no more than a few seconds, it is fading before your eyes and you *cannot* ignore it.

But there are other photographs which have to be searched for. You can find yourself in a place where you know there is a photograph, lurking as hidden as a fox in a thicket, which you can sense but not quite see. This glistening rock by a Pyrenean waterfall (below) was something it took most of an hour to find. I clambered around a stretch of hillside where a stream tumbled over a field of wet boulders. Finding a balance between the almost misty water and the great solidity of the stone – I was on the verge of giving up – was a sudden realisation that here was perfection in a looked-for moment, but a moment nonetheless of pure delight.

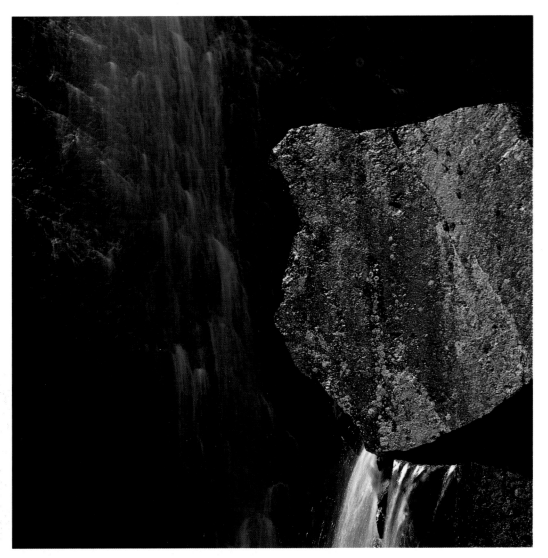

Parc National des Pyrénées-Occident, Pyrénées Atlantiques, France

So be both: both make the moment and take the moment, be acquisitive and absorbent, be patient and be quick.

Sometimes – and it is of course a rarity, something to be treasured and remembered – a landscape becomes in front of your eyes everything you ever hoped a landscape could be. This is difficult to describe as an experience, let alone to attempt to say how one might arrive at it. It is, of course, not something that can be engineered. Partly perhaps it is valuable because it is rare and can only be *given*, not sought or deliberately looked for. It is highly personal. All one can think is 'Yes, for me, what I see in front of me, what I am attempting to record, is what seems to me like a sort of revelation.' That must be the ultimate aim of landscape photography. Its business has to be revelation, in both its senses: a revealing of the

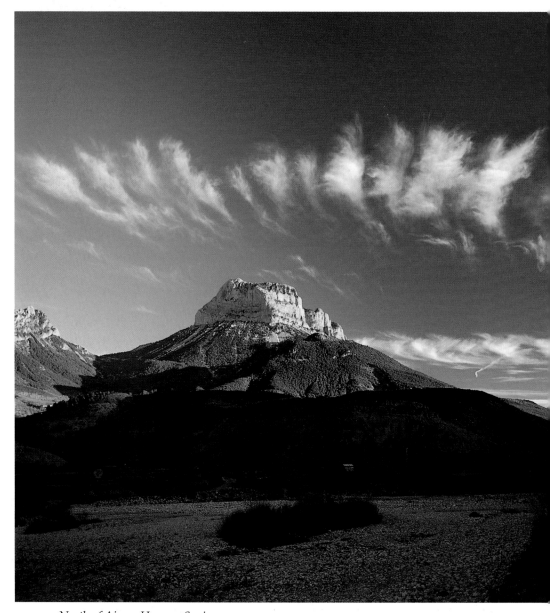

North of Ainsa, Huesca, Spain

Château Sully, Burgundy, France

material things that go to make up a place; and a channel through and beyond those things into the sort of realities which only revelation in its wider sense can give you access to.

In the body of this book you will find many specific 'Points to Watch' – what and what not to do, an analysis where I can make it of the many elements of the art, what I think I did right and where I went wrong. But it is important to remember that these things, the machinery of photography, are no more than a means to an end. It is easy enough – and a blind alley – to mistake those means for the end itself. That is the route of the man who knows so much about the woofers and tweeters on his hi-fi that he cannot listen to music. Perhaps I should say 'Beware the Points to Watch. They are not what it is about in the end.' But what, you might say, is it about? One is left with something alarmingly difficult to define – the sudden recognition of the beautiful. This either is or is not there. And when it is, the memory of it – and the photograph is nothing but a marvellously concrete form of memory, a denial of time which people before the last 150-odd years could only have dreamt of – is the priceless thing which we are all seeking.

The Arrangement of Parts

Organising the elements of a landscape is often the key to taking a good photograph. The themes in this chapter highlight the importance of making the most of what is there, knowing what to conceal or reveal, arranging the parts to create the best visual image and allowing the character of the landscape to speak for itself.

I WAS IN YORKSHIRE, in the Pennines. I stopped the car and felt the compulsion to go up to the brow of a little hill and look over. This is what I met on the far side: faultlessness staring me in the face. This impeccably maintained piece of landscape has the air of designed wholeness, a set-piece tableau in which every part might have been put there not with efficient farming in mind but the creation of a beautiful cloth, a perfect suit in which to clothe the earth. Everything works: the river provides a good thick generous stripe along the bottom of the picture; the liquid curve of the track that sweeps up from the bridge is fitted sweetly into the shapes of the hill (sweetly in the sense that a ball will sing effortlessly and cleanly away from

the sweet spot on a bat). The walls step back into the distance with a regularity and sharpness that is as satisfying as the precise interlocking noises made by the shutter as it opens and closes. The barns punctuate the picture, pinning it down, giving it an exact sense of scale.

It is a marvellous order. There is no uncertainty here. Everything is congruent with everything else. It is a picture of complete but relaxed control, as pleasing as a mown lawn scattered with the sort of eyecatchers with which an eighteenth-century grandee would have decorated his park.

This photograph is simply a recognition of what is there. The farmers and builders of Swaledale have done all the work.

16

UPPER SWALEDALE, WEST YORKSHIRE

Film: Ektachrome 64 ASA
Camera: 6 x 6 centimetres
Lens: Short telephoto
Exposure: 1/2 second at f.32
Filter: Polarising

POINT TO WATCH

● *In a big landscape such as this, watch out for the direction of the light. Here it is from the side, lighting the end walls of the little barns and throwing their faces into shadow. This is important because it makes the buildings substantial and three-dimensional. Sun coming from behind the camera would light the front walls and throw the side walls into shadow. They might then have looked simply like stage flats and the reality of this amazing scene would have been reduced.*

The Graphic Image

SOUTH OF SIENA, TUSCANY

Perhaps the landscape is at its simplest and most shapely, when the elements within it are almost graphic. If the landscape seems to be drawn, then you can be sure that it has the makings of a photograph.

Of all forms of agriculture, the vine is perhaps the most tightly controlled. To respond to that, the photograph must join in with the spirit of its subject. The elements must repeat as they do here. Anything – such as the sky – that distracts from the purity of the graphic image must be excluded. Even the posts at the bottom are a distraction. Put your hand over them to cut them out and see how it improves the picture.

Once the picture has established this simplicity, there is a great deal to be said for returning it to some of the idiosyncrasies of the real world. That is why the ripple in the vines at the back give a visual twist to the picture, a flip of reality, without which it might have dried up into a diagram.

Film: Fujichrome 50 ASA
Camera: 6 x 6 centimetres
Lens: Telephoto
Exposure: 1/2 second at f.45
Filter: Polarising

POINTS TO WATCH

● *Use a long lens to compress everything, flattening a landscape into a graphic pattern.*
● *Simplicity of pattern needs to be matched by simplicity – and strong contrast – in colour. Here the presence of only two colours strengthens the photograph.*

The key to this picture is the placing of the trees in a line along the foot of the frame. This breaks all the conventional rules of composition, which insist that the main focus of interest in a picture should come a third or two-thirds of the way into it. But to put them here was obvious to me from the start. There was a large expanse of green field at the bottom of the picture and to have included that within the frame would have distracted all one's attention away from the string of little globes that line the boundary between the grass and the dark of the hillside in the background.

I have tried to make the pattern clear by allowing the little pom-poms to dominate. They can only do so if they are allowed to be the most vibrant moment in the frame.

NORTH OF VALENCE, VERCOURS

Film: Fujichrome 50 ASA
Camera: 6 x 6 centimetres
Lens: Telephoto
Exposure: 1 second at f.45
Filter: Polarising

POINTS TO WATCH

● *A weak sky might have been removed from the top of the photograph. It distracts attention from the pom-poms of the trees.*

● *The light coming into the trees from the back casts big clean pools of shadow in front of them. Crisp cast shadows like this always add three-dimensionality to photographs and help 'point out' the line of trees.*

● *If I could have arranged it, I would have preferred greater separation between the trees, especially at the edges of the frame, where individual trees should not be cut in two.*

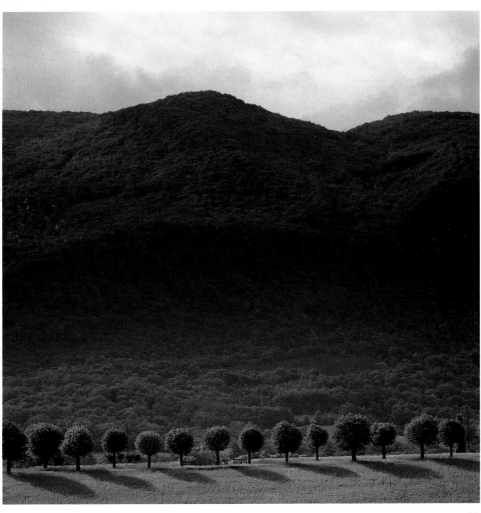

Perfect Balance

NEAR MARTEL, LOT

This picture always confuses people. The first reaction is always 'You've stuck two pictures together.' But I haven't. This is how it was. It always pleases me when I look at it that the division down the middle follows right through to the back of the scene, picked up by the fence in the distance. The sense of balance – or perhaps one should see it as complete imbalance – has a time element in it too. This has all the appearance of a before-and-after picture, although it was captured in a single moment. A friend once said to me that it has 'the appealing strangeness of a real scene.' I like to think of it as the landscape playing games.

Film: Ektachrome 64 ASA
Camera: 6 x 6 centimetres
Lens: Wide-angle
Exposure: 1/2 second at f.22
Filter: Polarising

POINTS TO WATCH

● *Ideally the sky should be bland. The blue is intrusive and so are the clouds. The perfectionist would have returned another day. But if the sky had been bland, there would have been no shadows and the picture would have suffered.*
● *The polarising filter has been used to deepen the green of the oats. The pay-off for that is no light in the shadows.*

20

THE COVE, AVEBURY, WILTSHIRE

Of course the landscape rarely provides you with as clear-cut a symmetry as the field in Martel (opposite). Usually the balancing of the elements within a picture is subtler, takes longer and involves a series of intuitive judgements.

These Neolithic standing stones at Avebury in Wiltshire are a case in point. What works here is the bringing of two very different things into a satisfactory relationship with each other. The large wide stone seen edge on and the plate of rock on the left are visually as different as Morecambe and Wise, but they complement each other: a balance not of equivalents but of opposites.

The tree in the background delineates the horizon and fills the gap between the stones. The effect – and this is something you have to feel your way towards – is of objects arranged with care and attention.

Film: Ektachrome 64 ASA
Camera: 6 x 6 centimetres
Lens: Wide-angle
Exposure: 1/4 second at f.22
Filter: None

POINTS TO WATCH

● *The very soft lighting, almost without shadow, reveals the texture of the stones. Something much more harshly lit would have thrown the photograph out of kilter. Remember that highlights and shadows will always play the role of additional objects in the landscape. An arrangement of parts made in one set of lighting conditions is unlikely to work in another.*

● *This is a classic instance of not snatching at a view. The role of the background tree is crucial here, but it took a while to realise that. Never forget the details. On them the balance will tip.*

The Lighter Touch

LAC D'IRATI, PYRENEES-ATLANTIQUES

The arrangement of parts discussed so far in this section has been a question of rather strict formality. But the principles at work in those strictly arranged photographs are still relevant even when the landscape presents a looser and baggier face.

This lake is high in the French Pyrenees, where the luxuriant beech wood is one of the marvels of Europe, dripping with early-morning dew like a freshly washed salad.

Formality has been allowed to relax here, but you can still feel the structure of the place. This is helped by the most simple of structural elements – the reflection of the arc in the waters of the lake. You might think that, with all that is going on at the right-hand side, it would become unbalanced, but the reflection compensates for this.

Cut that out with your hand and you will see how the whole picture slumps to the left. There is no need for complete symmetry.

Film: Ektachrome 64 ASA
Camera: 6 x 6 centimetres
Lens: Wide-angle
Exposure: 1/8 second at f.16/f.22
Filter: Polarising, half-polarised

POINT TO WATCH

● *The image of the sky reflected in the water is more interesting than the sky itself, because less light is reflected off the water and the exposure can pick up the variations of light and shade. A grey graduated filter over the sky would have reduced the brightness to that of the reflected image and improved the picture.*

PIC D'IRATI, PYRENEES-ATLANTIQUES

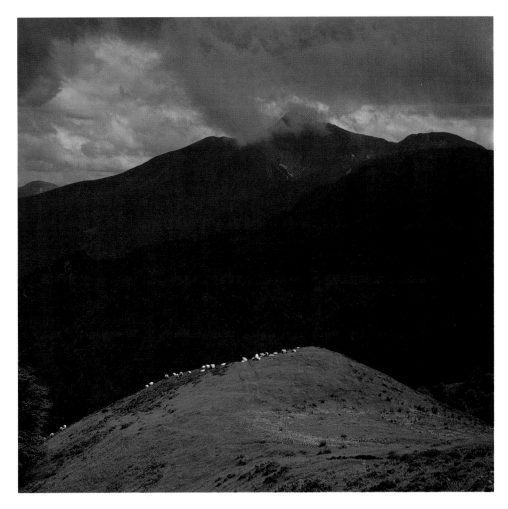

This photograph was taken the following day. There was hardly any sun, only the odd flash of light creeping through the clouds. The picture would not have worked unless the sheep had been there, marking the edge of the hill. They give life to the whole scene. The mountain background, which is dark and inanimate, is brought right up against the lit and living rim of the hill. The flock is crucial to the picture because it delineates the elements within it. This is a dramatisation of the elements in the landscape, perhaps in the same way as the photograph on page 11, where the white blossom and the white snow bridges the distances that separate parts of the mountain world. But again, the control is not rigid here. The flock is no more than a light flick with the point of the brush, something slight in a landscape of great size and visual violence. This is not a photograph cramped by strict graphical control. (Consider how far it is from the vines on page 18.) But perhaps this slightness of control in a picture is, in the end, more satisfying.

Film: Ektachrome 64 ASA
Camera: 6 x 6 centimetres
Lens: Short telephoto
Exposure: 1/4 second at f.32
Filter: None

POINT TO WATCH

● *I would have preferred the sheep at the very bottom left of the frame not to be there . They muddle the clarity of the picture's idea. But photography is certainly one of the arts of the possible and stage direction of sheep is not – yet – one of my skills.*

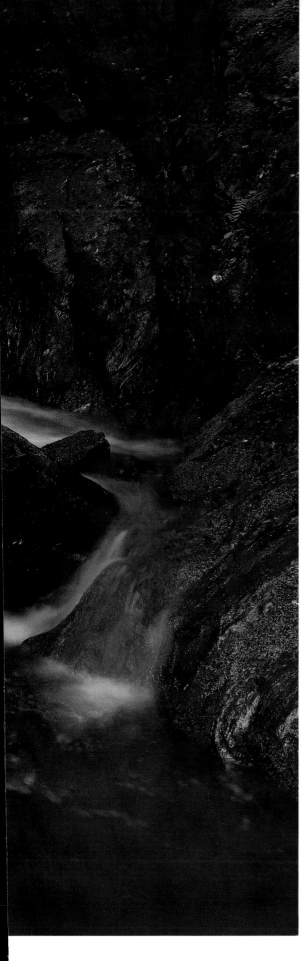

Making the Picture Right

WATERFALL AT LAC D'AUBERT, PYRENEES

I want to describe the stages by which this picture was taken. I was driving along the shore of a lake. The road crossed a bridge over a mountain stream and I stopped. The end of a waterfall, where it meets a lake or the sea, is usually the least interesting part. But there is always a point where the water falls vertically down the rock and I walked upstream looking for it. You need to have a picture in mind, but you must also be open to the landscape and alert to its opportunities.

Once I had found the place came the long process of selection to make the picture right. This picture is close up to its subject. If I had moved further out, it would have included the untidy woodland to left and right; in fact, I am not entirely happy with the bits of green on the right. I wish that there were only two colours in the picture – those of the rock and the water. But to have gone in any closer, removing the green, would have lost the gush of water on the left. Block that side out with your hand and you will see how the picture is diminished.

There was equally little choice about the upper and lower limits. The lowest point of the log-like rock needs to be there, as does the point where the stream emerges at the top. Hold your hand across either of those two, and the point of the picture is lost.

Film: Fujichrome 50 ASA
Camera: 6 x 6 centimetres
Lens: Wide-angle
Exposure: 2 seconds at f.22
Filter: 81b warm-up

POINTS TO WATCH

● *The rock face to the right of the fall in the background was already glistening with spray. But the large face to the left was dry and unreflective. So I splashed it with water from the stream to make it shine. Never hesitate to make temporary changes to the scene in front of you.*
● *I used a long exposure to soften the water and make it silky. This also revealed the structure of the water's movement down the fall.*

The Chosen Space

RIVER DOVEY, POWYS

I was faced with a choice here, the sort of
choice on which the whole art of
photography hinges. These two photographs
were taken one after another, with no
horizontal movement of the camera. One is
simply lifted higher than the other. There is
no doubt in my mind which one works best;
it is the picture above covering acres of sky.
It may be because there is a technical
pleasure in it. You can hardly ever

Film: Ektachrome 64 ASA
Camera: 6 x 6 centimetres
Lens: Short telephoto
Exposure: 1/4 second at f.32
Filters: High-density grey graduated; 81b warm-up

photograph sun except at the very end of
the day. Here, because of the particular half-
transparent clouds, I could get a picture of it
high in the sky, its tiny disk no bigger than

RIVER DOVEY, POWYS

a fingernail. You can see why in Ancient Athens when scientists calculated that the sun was slightly bigger than the Peloponnese, they were generally thought to be mad.

That is the sort of satisfaction that comes not from a photograph but from the actual process of photographing it. It should not in the end govern one's ideas about a picture.

But the reasons for my preferring the 'sky' picture to the river picture are quite straightforward: the sky is so much more interesting to look at. The dazzle of the reflected sunlight is more dramatic than the flatter light of the picture above, and the patterns of light and dark far more dynamic. It is the difference between an ordinary somewhere and a place you might travel miles to visit – a difference made by tilting the camera five or ten degrees.

Film: Ektachrome 64 ASA
Camera: 6 x 6 centimetres
Lens: Short telephoto
Exposure: 1/4 second at f.32
Filters: High-density grey graduated; 81b warm-up

POINTS TO WATCH

● *Tilt the camera by as little as five or ten degrees to achieve a completely different picture.*
● *A massive grey graduated filter was necessary to 'bring in' the sky. Without it the sky would have been enormously overexposed. The way to judge the strength of graduation that is needed is to look at the sky with your eyes half shut. If you can only do so with your eyes virtually closed then you need a heavy one. If you can look more wide-eyed at the sky, then a lighter filter will be all right. This gets easier with experience.*

A Place in its Place

BARMOUTH, GWYNEDD

Film: Ektachrome 64 ASA
Camera: 6 x 6 centimetres
Lens: Short telephoto
Exposure: 1/2 second at f.32
Filter: Low-density grey graduated

Again, a single place provides its choices. I far prefer the picture on the opposite page to the one below. The mass of mountain in the background is so much greater and makes the Victorian building look, as it surely was intended to, much more vulnerable than it does below.

I thought at first that a notched and craggy outline to the hills behind would make more of an impact, imposing the mountain presence more forcibly on everything below it than a flat horizon could do.

But then I moved to the position from which the picture opposite was taken. Look first at the differences in the water of the estuary. It is both more patterned and somehow more serene than in the earlier picture. The black utterly unlit hump of land in the distance and the way the water stretches continuously towards it give one a greater sense of distance and dimension. It is a grander picture, the grandeur surrounding the sweetness of a Victorian house squeezed between the mountains and the sea.

POINTS TO WATCH

● *The lower light in the picture on page 28 means that the exposure is a little darker.*
● *Consider carefully what it is that you need from a photograph and then go out to find it. You can actively seek it.*

Film: Ektachrome 64 ASA
Camera: 6 x 6 centimetres
Lens: Short telephoto
Exposure: 1/2 second at f.32
Filter: Low-density grey graduated

BARMOUTH, GWYNEDD

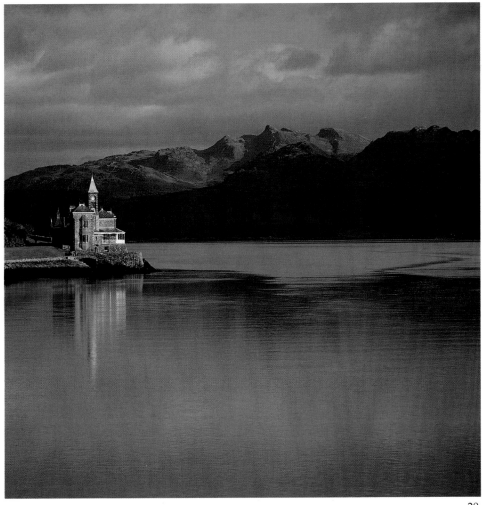

Simplicity

The simplest photographs are often the most successful. This chapter shows how, by seeking simplicity in the landscape – either by isolating a single object or by reducing a natural scene to a few interlocking elements – a pattern emerges, and a strong visual effect can be achieved.

I AM WALKING along the salt-marsh lawn on the edge of a river estuary in Normandy. The river is a plane of glass. The morning is cold but brightly lit, a perfect clarity in the air. Then this, a fishing boat hauled out on to the bank, its shape, colour and setting all perfect. The picture made itself.
I changed only one element in the scene, letting the chain, which had been curled up inside the boat, hang down towards the mud. Why did I do that? I'm not sure. It quite simply seemed better that way, visually attching the prow of the boat to the ground on which it rested.
But that chain is symptomatic of something that is critical in a photograph like this, where the main outlines of the picture are quite straightforward. And that is the all-

important role played by what seem to be comparatively unimportant elements.There are several here without which the picture would fall apart. Hold your thumb over the brightly lit patch of mud left of the boat; and then over the bright transom on the right. As you do so, you see meaning and coherence drop away. Even stranger is the part played by the rather shapeless clouds at the top. Block them out with your hand and the picture becomes unbalanced, full of too much grass. To make it work again you have to cut away most of that grass in the foreground, but then the image becomes pinched and the boat is not given its place in the landscape.
It is one of those photographs from which nothing can happily be removed.

THE ESTUARY OF THE SEE, AVRANCHES, MANCHE

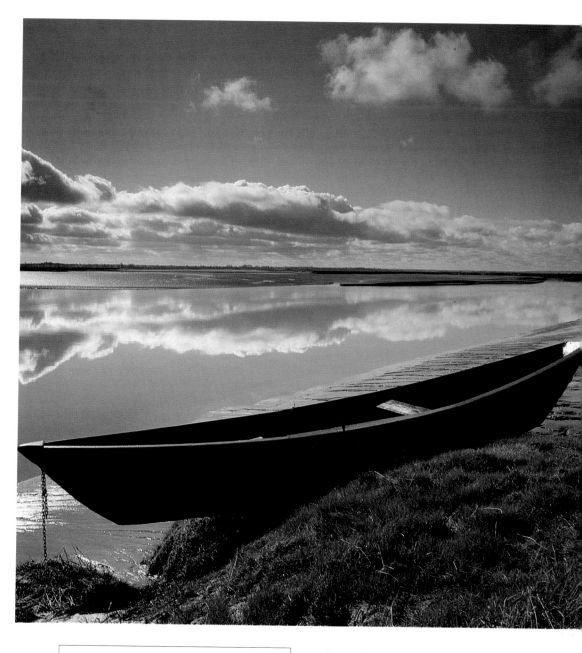

Film: Ektachrome 64 ASA
Camera: 6 x 6 centimetres
Lens: Standard
Exposure: 1 second at f. 22
Filter: Polarising, fully polarised

POINTS TO WATCH

● *In a backlit picture, look out for direct light falling onto the lens, which causes flare.*
To prevent this, shade the lens with your hand or a lens-hood.

● *Harsh sunlight leads to loss of detail in the shadows, but if the composition is strong, don't worry. High contrast, in fact, improves the image, pushing it towards an abstract.*
● *With close-ups, be careful about the foreground. The picture could have been improved if I had taken a little more care by cleaning away the dead grasses and scattering loose grass on the patch of white clay on the left. This would have both clarified and balanced the photograph.*

A Single Remark

EAST OF CORDOBA, ANDALUCIA

Put your thumb over the trees in the picture above and what do you get? An advertisement for the Ukraine in the Soviet Agricultural Weekly. Of course the barley is beautiful, in that perfect midway stage between green and gold, a month or so before it is ripe and harvested. But without the trees the picture degenerates into a bore.

There is no great mystery to this: isolate anything and that very isolation will make it more important.

This may be an easy thing to do but it is not to be despised. It allows one to see something plainly, to hear a single note and to remove distraction. And what in the end can be the point of landscape photography but to see something properly and for itself?

Film: Fujichrome 50 ASA
Camera: 6 x 6 centimetres
Lens: Wide-angle
Exposure: 1/4 second at f.22
Filters: Polarising, fully polarised; 81c warm-up; low-density grey graduated

POINTS TO WATCH

● *There was no wind when I took this picture. This was absolutely necessary to get the definition in the ears of the barley, as a relatively long exposure was needed for the depth of field.*
● *A deep dark sky would have been wrong. This is a breezy light picture and all the colours needed to conform to that.*
● *A mild warm-up filter was used to emphasise the yellow latent in the barley.*

EAST OF SINALUNGA, TUSCANY

I love this picture of the single tree. It is an image of utter solitude against a grey bank of cloud, a single remark dropped into a virtual silence.

Perhaps it is more what surrounds the tree than the tree itself that makes this photograph – the beautiful opening sky after rain, and beneath it the softened colours of the evening landscape, each colour folding into the next. It is, for me, like one of those moments of which only great music is capable, when the mood subtly alters from violence to a new and washed calm. The solid presence of the tree is needed to fix that moment.

Film: Fujichrome 50 ASA
Camera: 6 x 6 centimetres
Lens: Wide-angle
Exposure: 1 second at f.22
Filter: 81b warm-up

POINTS TO WATCH

● *Always watch out for litter. You cannot tidy it out of the picture later. I should have tidied up the foreground here more than I did.*

● *It would have been absolutely wrong to put the tree in the middle. It needs to be, even if almost unnoticeably, a little off to one side. I am not sure why, but I often offset a main subject slightly to the right.*

The Complete Picture

I ALWAYS TRY to recreate in a photograph the feeling you get when you suddenly see or hear something beautiful for the first time. It's the sensation of 'That's it! There is something perfect', the feeling that raises the hairs on the back of the neck. I don't know what it is that produces this sensation, but one part of it is certainly the impression of completeness, that something has been caught whole and nothing is left unexplained.

NEAR S. GIMIGNANO, TUSCANY

Here, the evening light with its long shadows and almost sculptural separation of foreground from background creates a rich textured shape which the flatter light of midday would not have achieved. As it is, the light reveals the place. The single tree is a necessary accent. (Cover it with a finger to understand its importance). But one extra element makes the picture complete; the wind on the valley side in the middle distance has ruffled the grasses, softening them as though the valley is coated in the fur of a cat. There is unexpectedness in that, introducing a subtle air of movement.

Film: Fujichrome 50 ASA
Camera: 6 x 6 centimetres
Lens: Standard
Exposure: 1/2 second at f.22
Filter: 81b warm-up

POINTS TO WATCH

● *Use amber warm-up filters to emphasise the golden light of evening.*
● *Remove the sky from a photograph to maintain overall control of the colour range.*
● *The little patch of green on the left of the frame is to my mind a fault in the photograph. It could not be avoided; immediately to the right was a large field of bright green wheat.*

NEAR RONDA, ANDALUCIA

CAMARGUE

The air of completeness in this picture is achieved by almost exactly the opposite means of the previous one. Here every element stands out in complete distinction from the rest: each of the four colours is almost undilutedly itself; the hill, trees and sky are pure blocks of colour. In the Tuscan photograph every element complements and enhances the others; here the whole is made by the bringing of sharp opposites together. The Tuscan photograph *suggests* completeness, this one demonstrates the clarity of trees on a white hill under a blue sky.

A third way of achieving this air of completion is this; the single receding structure. There is nothing complicated about the picture. Blue and yellow are at opposite ends of the spectrum and to bring them so closely together enhances both colours. The polarising filter deepens all colours, particularly the blue of the sky, but that adds little to what is there anyway. I love this picture, partly because it is so simple. When something is as perfectly complete in itself as this, then the photographer can, or should, have little to add.

Film: Fujichrome 50 ASA
Camera: 6 x 6 centimetres
Lens: Short telephoto
Exposure: 1/30 second at f.11
Filter: Polarising, half-polarised

Film: Fujichrome 50 ASA
Camera: 6 x 6 centimetres
Lens: Wide-angle
Exposure: 1/2 second at f.22
Filter: Polarising, fully polarised

POINTS TO WATCH

● *The photograph would not work without the cloud, which in some ways mirrors the texture of the field. Always wait for the sky to come right.*
● *The midday light creates only very black shadows under the trees. In these conditions look for 'false shadows', as from the colours in the earth of the field, to give shape to the landscape.*
● *Avoid the mistake I made here with the tree on left, which emerges from the hill without its trunk.*

POINTS TO WATCH

● *The polariser, to darken the sky, eliminates much of the reflection of the reeds in the foreground. This is simply a choice one has to make; I felt more was gained this way than lost.*
● *The great depth of field necessary to bring the whole line of reeds into focus made a long exposure necessary and a couple of reeds are blurred in the wind. Ideally, I should have waited even longer for complete stillness.*

Reducing a Picture to Match its Subject

Islay, Inner Hebrides

A single object – a boat, a swan, a tree – always works in a photograph, no matter where it is. It is both an image of romantic isolation and a picture of simplicity. And that itself is a pleasure to look at, reducing what you see to a single meaning, shutting out extraneous things because they have no business being there, a vision of something pure and simple when usually what you get in your view of the world is a buzz of disorganised information, the every-day restlessness of things. The single object in a wide expanse is the embodiment of calm.

But there is a danger. The lonely object may be too lonely. It may actually disappear into the picture it is attempting to control. I think that might be a problem with the uncropped frame here. But there are also other things at work, all of which need sorting out. First, to have the horizon coming halfway up the picture is a mistake because dividing the picture-space precisely in two is a formula for imbalance – the two halves struggle too equally with each other. I could have pointed the camera higher into the sky, but higher up, on this evening, the sky was losing its beautiful mottling. Even in the upper reaches of the photograph as I took it the clouds have started to get too light and lose their texture. But there is a solution to these difficulties. In fact, this is an occasion where the true meaning of the photograph is revealed only by cropping it quite radically, reducing the landscape to the simple and evocative width of a panorama. The boat, simply by occupying a larger proportion of the picture space, has taken control of it. The beautiful and very slight ripples in the lit water on the left-hand side become visible for the first time.

Film: Fujichrome 50 ASA
Camera: 6 x 6 centimetres
Lens: Ultra wide-angle
Exposure: 2 seconds at f.22
Filter: Polarising

POINT TO WATCH

● *Control of the horizon is quite obviously completely critical here. Check it with a spirit level after every exposure.*

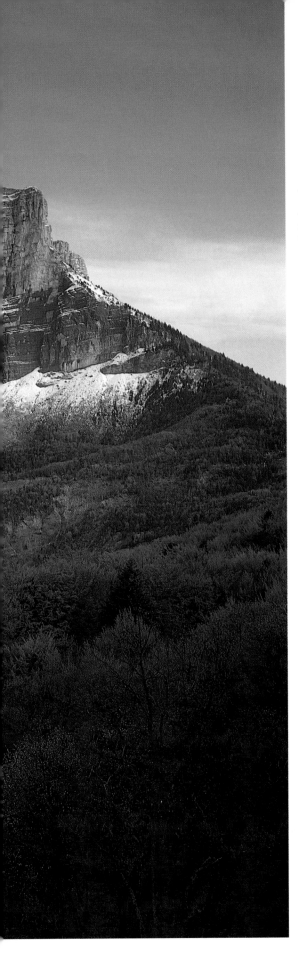

The Monumental Object

MONT GRANIER, SAVOIE

Here, quite simply, the whole landscape has become a single object, so that the mountain stands like a sculpture on a plinth. The limestone massif dominates the place and the job of excluding distractions is already done magnificently, monumentally, for you.

Various other elements are highly important to the success of the picture. It would not have been enough to point a camera at a big lump of rock and hope for this atmosphere of massive dominance.

The lighting conditions happened to be perfect, slowly changing in the finest gradations from the deep shadow at the bottom right to the climax of the lightest part of the stone face. The fine scatter of snow over the high rock works as a sort of artificial highlight.

This is a subtle effect, the tones working with the geometry of the picture, but it is important. The light establishes, probably subliminally, the huge emergence of the mountain above the valley. Without it there would have been far less *intelligibility* in the landscape, little to lead you from foreground to background. The mountain, at least in these terms, would have been inaccessible.

All this is helped by the simplicity of the light. It is almost shadowless, very late in the evening and the photograph is taken with a long exposure. That too adds to the air of monumental calm.

Film:Fujichrome 50 ASA
Camera: 6 x 6 centimetres
Lens: Standard
Exposure: 1/2 second at f.22
Filters: None

POINTS TO WATCH

● *Lit snow remains white. If any of the snow had been sunk in shadow it would have gone blue and would have needed an 81-series warm-up filter to correct the colour.*
● *The mountain is pushed slightly to the right of centre. To have had it in the very middle would have destabilised the picture.*

Right Time, Right Place

Chance favours the prepared mind and both planning and luck play their part in creating a good photograph. Think ahead, prepare for the weather conditions you might expect and remember, for example, that big views are almost always better in the morning and evening. But also take advantage of the unexpected and be prepared to experiment.

WHEN I ARRIVED in this field it was winter, perhaps late autumn. It was 6.30 in the morning and the field was empty. I was taken not with any particular element in the landscape in front of me but with the way that everything here fitted with everything else: the softening early-morning light, the mist coming off the grass, the way in which colour was drained out of everything. The cows wandered in from somewhere off left.

As I think one can see in the photograph, if you look at it carefully, analytically and ungenerously, the actual elements in the picture are not that attractive. The houses are dull and the church too stern. At another time of day I would not have bothered with the place at all. But here, with a light mist

that takes out the colour but allows detail to remain in both the buildings and the sky, it was a picture worth getting up for.

And that is a phrase of which, if you pursue photography with any seriousness, you will continue to remind yourself. The light of mid-morning, noon and afternoon is rarely the light that will reveal the nature of a place. Low light, whether at evening or early morning, will always find its way into the corners and create the sculptural shadows that a photograph needs.

But it is not simply revelation that you are after here. Concealment, the suggestiveness of low light, the simplicity of the light before dawn, perfect in its grey shadowlessness: these are the circumstances in which good pictures will happen.

40

STROSSWIHR, NEAR MUNSTER, VOSGES

Film: Fujichrome 50 ASA
Camera: 6 x 6 centimetres
Lens: Wide-angle
Exposure: 1 second at f.22
Filters: 81b warm-up

POINTS TO WATCH

● *Don't ever allow the point of a steeple to interrupt a skyline. Use a ladder to keep the tip of the steeple within the hill in the background.*
● *With a flock or herd of animals try not to have them masking one another, but distinct as they are here. A full, patterned spread will always look best.*
● *The house and the animal's bottom at the far left should be cut out. Always go for clarity; make the meaning clear.*

The Revealing Winter

WEST OF CELANO, ABRUZZI

In the very middle of the winter at the end of the afternoon, I can feel myself still being invited into this picture. It makes you want to walk into it, doesn't it? I would like to tell you, as I know it looks, that this upland valley, high in the Apennines, was rigid with frost at the time. It wasn't; I was rather hot, in shirtsleeves.

But everything about it speaks the Mediterranean winter. It is sharp at every point. Nothing is muffled or clothed. Trees, soil and mountain are all naked. At any other time of year the trees would have concealed each other and the distant mountains – that all-important baseline against which the things near at hand need to be set – would have been invisible. This is the revealing winter in which the low light and long shadows reveal the texture and nature of the rocky soil as if the nap on a cloth has been raised. Landscape photography is not only for the summer. In some ways it comes into its own when looking at the bare bones of winter.

Film: Fujichrome 50 ASA
Camera: 6 x 6 centimetres
Lens: Ultra wide-angle
Exposure: 1/8 second at f.22
Filter: 81c warm-up

POINTS TO WATCH

● *I should really have stepped back a few yards to try to encompass the trees in the foreground, not to clip them at the edges. In a photograph where the whole point is clarity and revelation, try to ensure that shapes remain whole.*
● *I have wondered if the use of the 81c warm-up filter is too much here. It is necessary to take the blue out of the shadows on the snow but is the effect now too yellow?*
● *Try to achieve a formal balance between the foreground and background which is satisfying. Here I feel the relative weights of tree and mountain are about right.*

The Investigating Light of Evening

NEAR MELROSE, BORDERS

What is this picture about? It is of course the meeting of two fields and two colours, separated by a single low wall. It is a simple pattern, a classic instance in fact of a landscape becoming attractive through the reduction of information. But this photograph would not have been half what it is here if it had been taken in the more vertical and whiter light of the middle of the day. Here the low, raking light of evening makes – through the large shadow – the substance of the wall much more real. The low light is the only set of conditions in which the full potential of the place could be completely realised. The long lens, as always, has led to a loss of definition, but in a picture of such warmth and larger blocky effects, this is not important.

Film: Ektachrome 64 ASA
Camera: 6 x 6 centimetres
Lens: Telephoto
Exposure: 1 second at f.22
Filters: None

POINTS TO WATCH

● *This is a cropped photograph. A great deal of the foreground which would have distracted from the main point of the picture has been eliminated.*
● *Block out the sky with your hand to show how the yellow becomes the most important patch in the photograph, tightening the picture up. Would cropping the sky out improve it?*
● *The colours in the evening are much richer than in the middle of the day. The depth of green is almost too much. Perhaps a little earlier in the evening would have suited the place more.*

SOUTH OF SIENA, TUSCANY

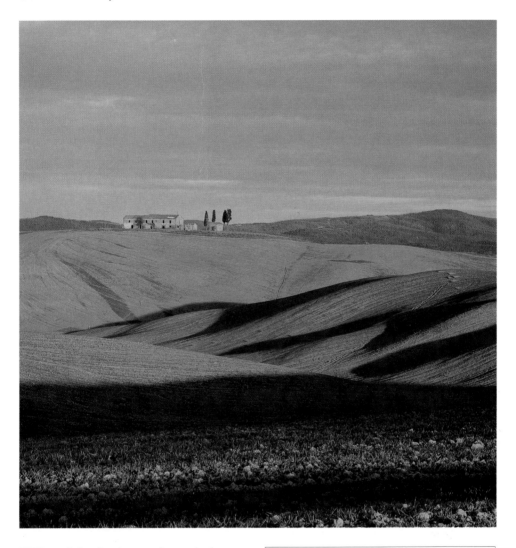

The subtler the shapes of a particular piece of country the more investigative the light needs to be. The fine modulations of a gently billowing field only emerge in light that glances off the rounded ridges and throws the troughs between them into shadow. It is a stroking light which flatters by attending to the shapes on which it falls.

The effect of the evening light on the little ruined house is interesting. It is set much more certainly within its neighbouring landscape than it would have been earlier in the day. Imagine this scene without the swell of the landscape revealed. The house would be set adrift in a sea of fields. You wouldn't in some senses know where it was, and any loss of information is a loss to the photograph.

Film: Ektachrome 64 ASA
Camera: 6 x 6 centimetres
Lens: Telephoto
Exposure: 1 second at f.32
Filters: Polarising

POINTS TO WATCH

● *The light and shadow in the foreground share the quality of light and shadow in the distance. On the principle of always explaining as much as you can, it is always worth trying to reproduce in the foreground what is happening in the distance. Imagine a foreground entirely bathed in shadow. The picture would have become quite unbalanced.*

● *It is lucky that there is a greyish sky. A fierce blue sky would have stolen the show from what was happening on the ground.*

The Dramatics at the End of the Day

CHATEAU CHAMBORD, LOIRE

I feel a little ambivalent about Chambord. It's rather a mother-in-law of a chateau, isn't it? You might fall in love with somewhere like Azay-le-Rideau, but this is really a little too much, the architecture of the really fulsome *embonpoint*. Nevertheless I feel sure that the men who built it must have had this photograph in mind. Coming here is like arriving in a theatre. Every decision has already been taken for you. The architects and landscapers have created a set in which the last of the sun provides the supremely appropriate lighting. The building is such an overstatement that only in the little light of evening can the vast airless bulk begin to look beautiful, the duchess at the ball, her jewels sparkling about her.

Film: Fuijichrome 50 ASA
Camera: 6 x 6 centimetres
Lens: Wide-angle
Exposure: 1 second at f.22
Filter: Polarising, half-polarised

POINTS TO WATCH

● *Shadow at the end of the day comes in very fast indeed. This, if anything, is a little too late. On the right-hand tower the dark has already climbed a third of the way up the building. With evening photography make sure that you get there in very good time.*
● *The polarising filter will take more light out of the water than the sky. With reflected buildings this works well, framing the reflection you want by killing the reflections in the foreground.*

46

ALBI, TARN

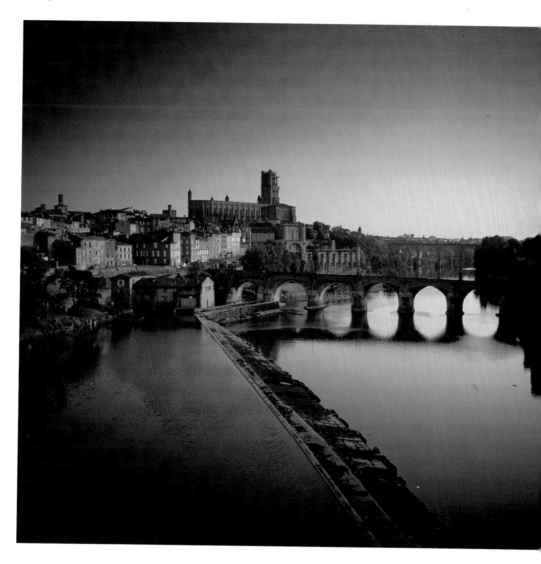

I arrived at Albi at the end of a long day. I was not interested in taking a picture here: there was no light left to speak of; and I had switched off, thinking only of somewhere to stay. And then this. I was caught unawares by it, by the city presenting itself at its absolute best.

Light can lie. Albi is not on the whole a very attractive town, but light as theatrical as this is so seductive and flattering that no human being would be allowed to get away with it. But the photographer is in a position to use all the cosmetics of evening light to make a place seem astonishing.

The light here is so directional, and there is little of it, lighting only the best part of the houses – the river frontage – so that, oddly enough, more prominence in the picture is given to those houses than to the cathedral. The shutters add a little tang. And the light under the arches of the bridges helps.

Film: Fujichrome 50 ASA
Camera: 6 x 6 centimetres
Lens: Wide-angle
Exposure: 1 second at f.22
Filters: Polarising, fully polarised; 81c warm-up

POINTS TO WATCH

● *Perhaps the polarising filter has been over-used here. The bottom left-hand corner has lost all glow.*

● *81c warm-up filter I think was also over-used here. It should not be quite so red.*

Lenses

The lens is the medium through which the landscape reaches the film and almost nothing shapes a picture more radically than the choice of lens. The chapter discusses how and why standard, wide-angle and telephoto lenses might be appropriate in different situations.

THERE IS RARELY a question in my mind, when faced with a scene like this, about which lens to choose. It was obvious to me that only a wide-angle lens would make true sense of this seaside town. Why? Partly because the whole picture depends on the relationship of the promenade to the steps in front of them and any lens which was not wide enough would have cut that relationship in two. And to have done that would have been a waste of the marvellous tide-dampened sweep of the stepped seawall, which has something about it of the underside of a scallop shell.

The lens has also had the effect of making the promenade into quite an abstract picture. That is helped by the near-monochrome of the colours here, but also by what might be called the geometry of colour in it, the way in which the enormously wide 'arrows' of white houses, black steps and then the paler surface of the wet, light-reflecting steps, all diminish so sharply from the foreground to the disappearing point precisely in the centre of the picture. (It is significant, incidentally, that if all the steps had been wet and equally reflective, the picture would have lost a great deal of its impact. It needs that banding of black, white and black.)

None of this drama of recession would have been in the picture without using a wide-angle lens. A longer lens would have compressed and flattened the scene, clipping away the edges of the foreground and turning something that here I think looks dramatic into a dank and dreary morning on the north coast of Wales.

48

LLANDUDNO, GWYNEDD

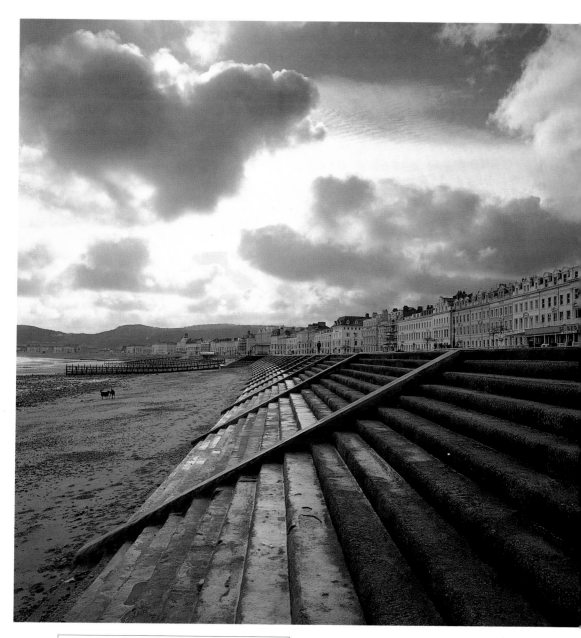

Film: Fujichrome 50 ASA
Camera: 6 x 6 centimetres
Lens: Wide angle
Exposure: 1 second at f.32
Filter: Low-density grey-graduated

POINTS TO WATCH

● *Watch out for flare in a backlit picture like this. Shield the lens with your hand or a hood but be careful that neither appears in the frame.*
● *If you are trying to include as much of a scene as possible – which can be the only*

justification for using a wide-angle lens – then it is vital that everything in the photograph is sharp. You need absolute maximum depth of field which means a long exposure. Make sure that the tripod is rock-steady and that the horizon is even.
● *Moving traffic would have spoilt the picture. If there had been a bus driving along the promenade, it would have here appeared as an ugly blur. Wait until there is no traffic, or better, as I did here, get up early. This was taken at about 7 am.*

The Better Picture

SOUTHWOLD, SUFFOLK

I was faced with this wonderful English scene. Southwold always seem to me stuck in 1956, and the row of all-too-English beach houses, stretching from here to eternity, cannot have changed for decades. How to photograph it? I started with the picture on the opposite page, well back on the beach with a wide-angle lens to take in the full length of the subject. But it is not a success. The graphic elements are too weak, the sky is a failure and there is far too much uninteresting and uninformative beach. The first instinct had been the wrong one.

I could simply have changed the wide-angle lens for a telephoto and come up with a picture something like the one above. But the following things would have happened.

Film: Fujichrome 50 ASA
Camera: 6 x 6 centimetres
Lens: Wide-angle
Exposure: 1/2 second at f.22
Filters: Polarising, fully polarised, 85 warm-up

The beach huts are above the level of the beach and I would have had to point the lens up and the verticals in the photograph would have begun to converge. The only way to have avoided that would have been to have climbed up a tall ladder. With a long lens it would also have been unlikely that the whole strip of beach huts would have been included in the frame.

The conclusion was obvious; I had to walk with the cameras and the wide-angle lens up to the the beach huts themelselves. Only then would I get both the large graphic shapes and the full length of the row.

● *In the close-up it is important to make sure that the verticals remain vertical. Do not tilt the camera up.*

● *Make sure you keep the whole row of huts in the picture opposite. Any slight movement even of one millimetre would have spoilt the composition. After each exposure check that the camera hasn't been jogged and the composition disrupted.*

● *In the close-up, the white hut dominates the picture too much. It would have been better*

halfway down the row of huts. At the moment its huge white bulk doesn't allow the other huts their full part. But the placing of the steps dictated this choice of position. Only here could they have had their full graphic impact.
The warm-up filter is used here to reduce the white.

● *The picture below could have been improved by cropping off the right-hand edge so that it just touched the end of the beach houses.*

Film: Fujichrome 50 ASA
Camera: 6 x 6 centimetres
Lens: Wide-angle
Exposure: 1/2 second at f.22
Filter: Polarising, fully polarised

SOUTHWOLD, SUFFOLK

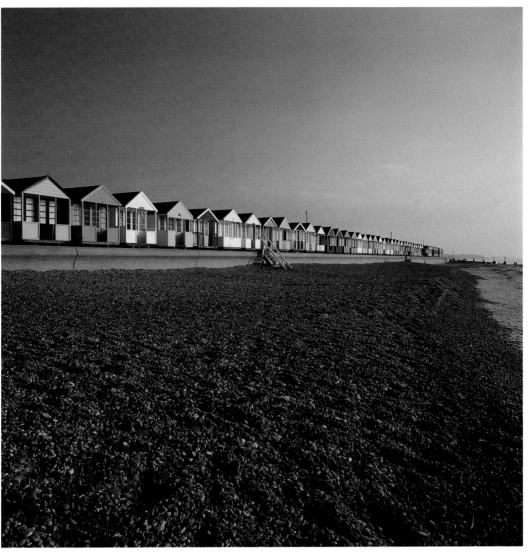

The Broader Space

SIDMOUTH, DEVON

This is not the scene that the people walking along the beach would have recognised. It was a bright day, not this strange and gloomy picture. But I knew I wanted to photograph the extraordinary mercury sheen on the wet beach and everything followed from that. It was clear that only a wide-angle lens would do. Always remember that a wide-angle lens works vertically as well as horizontally, bringing the photograph almost up to the feet of the photographer, so that in the reflections of the beach you are in effect photographing a large section of the sky. But it was necessary to bring down the light intensity of the sky to the level of the reflections on the beach. I had to put on two grey-graduated filters, a high- and a medium-density, to darken the sky sufficiently.

The result is that a sunny day is changed into something like a brightly lit storm. The fierce brightness on the sea is a necessary point of highly dramatic lighting, like the single point of light in the eye on a portrait, and the dark bulk of the cliffs anchors the whole composition. A standard lens could not hope for this effect, with a long lens you would not even have known the beach was wet.

Film: Fujichrome 50 ASA
Camera: 6 x 6 centimetres
Lens: Wide-angle
Exposure: 1 second at f.22
Filters: High-density grey-graduated and
medium-density grey-graduated

POINTS TO WATCH

● *The graduated filters have unfortunately cut into the top of the cliffs, overdarkening them.*
● *Check your horizon. Use a spirit level. An unstraight horizon would ruin a picture like this.*
● *When the sun is very low and you are photographing almost directly into it, flare – the result of sunlight falling directly on to the lens – is a danger. It could be that you will be forced to tilt your camera down and forsake your original intentions.*

Finding the Other Picture

NEAR LOGRONO, RIOJA, NAVARRA

There is always more than a single picture in a place. The temptation to include as much of this field of poppies as possible was almost overwhelming. It is the sheer spread of them that is so miraculous, the generous explosion of the natural world that they represent, set against the severe backdrop of the mountain in the distance. I wanted to make all I could of the colour of the poppies but to avoid the over-pretty effect of a deep blue sky. The combination of polarising filter, to raise the colour of the poppies, and grey-graduated filter to lower the intensity of the sky, works very well.

Much as I love this picture, there seemed to be something lurking in the landscape which it did not quite capture; the contrast between the harshness of the grey mountain and the richness of the meadow below it.

Film: Fujichrome 50 ASA
Camera: 6 x 6 centimetres
Lens: Wide-angle
Exposure: 1/2 second at f.22
Filters: Polarising, low-density grey-graduated

POINTS TO WATCH

● *For sharply defined foreground detail use a wide-angle lens.*
● *At slow shutter-speeds, any wind will blur flowers and grasses. Wait for a lull.*
● *To avoid under-exposing the middle distance, do not bring the grey-graduated filter too low. The top quarter of the picture is sufficient.*

A combination of waiting for the light to play over the scene in front of me and a change of lens produced this second image. I did not move the tripod a single inch.

A band of sunlight stripes the middle distance between the tree and the mountain. Both background and foreground are in shadow, so that the colour of the flowers is enriched by being slightly underexposed. The effect of a long lens is to bring the background closer to the foreground, so that the picture assumes a more concentrated form.

Its relationship to the longer view is clear; its impact could not be more different.

Film: Fujichrome 50 ASA
Camera: 6 x 6 centimetres
Lens: Short telephoto
Exposure: 1/4 second at f.22
Filters: Polarising, low-density grey-graduated

POINTS TO WATCH

● *A long lens can result in possible loss of resolution in the foreground. Ensure the smallest possible aperture for maximum depth of field.*
● *With a long lens, the possible depth of field is always reduced. Use a small step-ladder to get as high as possible above the foreground.*
● *The longer the lens, the less the definition.*

55

Excluding Distractions

KANONI, CORFU, GREECE

KANONI, CORFU, GREECE

It is quite clear which of these three pictures works the best: the one taken with the longest lens on the page opposite. The first, above, taken with the wide-angle lens, is weak because the information in every area of the picture is not strong enough to give it shape. The boats distract from the monastery and the monastery from the boats. It is too much of a 'scene', where a piece of this and that are tossed into the frame without any real care. Neither the root of the main jetty nor the jetty on the right hand side to which some further boats are moored are shown in this picture. It is a picture of incompleteness, an unshapely photograph from which elements have to be excluded to make it work.

The slightly longer lens is an improvement but it still doesn't work because the monastery, which is such a pretty building, demands to be seen more than it is shown here, because the sky continues to be boring and because the hills behind are poorly defined. This too is not yet a picture.

There is also a structural problem in that the island in the background competes with the monastery island for a dominant role in the picture so that one is left asking: what is this picture about?

Film: Fujichrome 50 ASA
Camera: 6 x 6 centimetres
Lens: Short telephoto
Exposure: 1/4 second at f.16
Filters: Polarising, 81d warm-up

Film: Fujichrome 50 ASA
Camera: 6 x 6 centimetres
Lens: Wide-angle
Exposure: 1/30 second at f.8
Filters: Polarising, 81d warm-up

POINTS TO WATCH

● *Consider the balance between the two islands. It would have been better if the far island was more to the left and the foreground island more to the right. To achieve this, I would have had to hover in mid air.*
● *Notice how in the bottom left of the picture the mast of a boat protrudes unexplained into the picture space. Always try to avoid unwanted intrusions like this.*

POINTS TO WATCH

● *Try not to cut boats in half as I have done here. Keep all the edges of a picture clean.*
● *When the sky is dull consider a photo that doesn't involve so much of it. An expanse of cloudless sky kills a picture*

The intense focus on the building with the long lens is the best. At last the one interesting thing in the picture is given its say. Even so here a little clipping of the edges of both the islands is annoying. I could perhaps have come in even closer with a longer lens but then the monastery would have been utterly removed from its context – a large part of its attraction lies in its island site – and the building would have been cramped. It is still not a completely pleasing picture, but this is a case where a long lens, simply by excluding the irrelevant, can transform a diaster of a photograph into one which at least has a certain allure.

Film: Fujichrome 50 ASA
Camera: 6 x 6 centimetres ce
Lens: Telephoto
Exposure: 1/2 second at f.22
Filters: Polarising, 81d warm-up

POINTS TO WATCH

● *Make sure when using a long lens that, for example, the little red boat here is not cut out. It provides the necessary bright pimple.*
● *It is important that there is no movement of wind or people. The meaning of the picture has to be still evening reflection, escpecially at this magnification. With a shorter lens, more 'noise' would have been livable with.*

KANONI, CORFU, GREECE

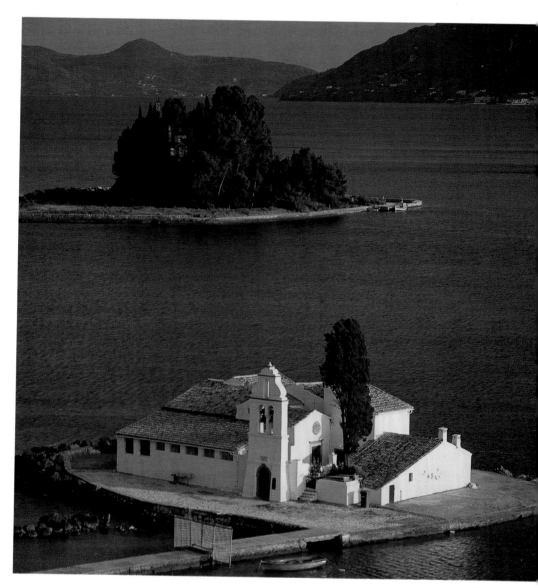

Movement and Exposure

A photograph is still and elements of the landscape are often mobile. That essential condition of the art means that decisions have to be made. Do you want to still the movement, wait for no movement or allow part of the picture to be blurred, either through the movement itself or by using a shallow depth of field? The chapter shows both the subtle and the extreme effects that changing the exposure can have.

I HAD A STRANGE and revealing experience with this photograph. It was on show in a gallery as part of an exhibition. An old lady with a monocle stood in front of the picture, had a good look at it and said, 'What a wonderful painting! Are you the artist?' I said I was.

It is worth asking why this picture seems to be such a painterly thing. First of all, it is to do with the quality of the light. I arrived here before the sun had come up; this is a photograph of the true light of dawn. The mist is going away and the colours are softened by the diffused light coming not from a single source but from the whole expanse of sky.

The low light required a long exposure and the absolute stillness of the reeds in the foreground, standing in the water as though they are painted one by one. It would not have been possible to have them like this if there had been any wind. Here is the essence of the still photograph.

There is something magical about this stilled stillness. It is a double effect, like cream poured over cream cheese, as though the landscape was existing already in the state of a photograph and the function of the photographer was to do no more than open his shutter and let the picture flood in. Of course, nothing could be further from the truth! Exquisite stillness demands even more control than usual. There could be no shooting off here. But precision picture making is the aspect of photography that gives me the most lasting pleasure.

RYDAL WATER, CUMBRIA

Film: Ektachrome 64 ASA
Camera: 6 x 6 centimetres
Lens: Wide-angle
Exposure: 1 second at f.32
Filters: None

POINTS TO WATCH

● *The structure of the picture is a series of layers which move back into the picture: the reeds, the shadow on the water, the trees on the left, the far woodland and finally the mountain in the distance, its base hidden by mist. The contours of these elements all droop in from the edges of the picture towards its centre, where the eye settles on the boathouse, the only sharp-edged object in the whole scene and its discreet if necessary focus.*

● *The photograph was taken on top of a stepladder. If I had been standing down at lake-level, very little of this, particularly in the foreground, would have worked: the reeds would not have been framed by the patch of lit water; the boathouse itself would not have been clear of them; and the patterning of successive layers in the picture would have been fatally compressed.*

Frozen Motion

VAL D'AMPOLA, LOMBARDY

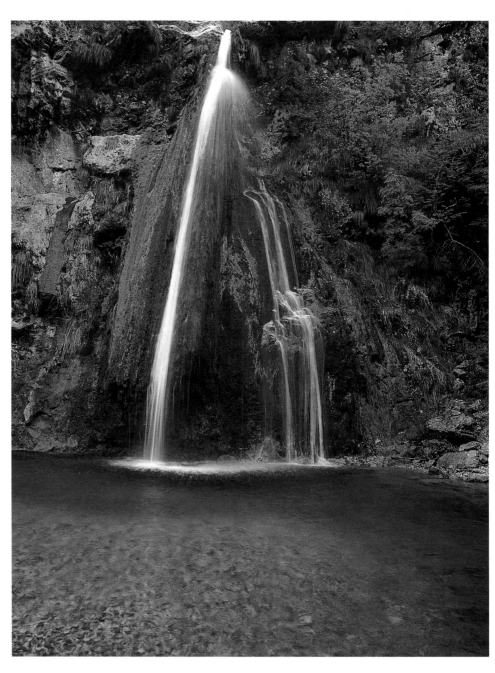

With moving water you have got a choice, you either freeze it or let it run. If you want to still water you have to use an exposure of not more than 1/30th of a second. But there is a lot to be said for allowing the movement in the water to appear in your frozen image of it. Time-blurred water has something of time buried

Film: Fujichrome 50 ASA
Camera: 6 x 6 centimetres
Lens: Wide angle
Exposure: 2 seconds at f.32
Filters: None

within it. But once you have decided to let the water move while the aperture is open, then you must decide how much are you going to let it run. How long an exposure do you want to give it? It is almost impossible to know at the time what the effect of a particular exposure will be on the water, but in general one or two seconds for fast flowing water is about right, depending on the lighting conditions. If you leave it a great deal longer than that, you are in danger of ending up with nothing but a white woolly

blur which wouldn't look like water. Always leave yourself with the choice afterwards, so bracket your exposures either side of one second. Two exposures under and two over will leave you with a sequence of photographs each achieving a slightly different effect.

Film: Fujichrome 50 ASA
Camera: 6 x 6 centimetres
Lens: Short telephoto
Exposure: 2 seconds at f.32
Filters: None

ARAN VALLEY, LERIDA, SPAIN

Depth of Field

WEST OF GUADALUPE, CACERES, SPAIN

I wanted to compress the scene, so that the tree played a large part in the picture. I couldn't get any closer because of the standing wheat in the field and so I had to use a very long lens. But the depth of field in a long lens is very small. To maximise it the smallest aperture had to be chosen. A very long exposure was necessary to compensate. Had there been no wind, this would have been no problem, but two seconds allows wind to make itself felt and show its effect on a picture. So you can see in the picture where the wind has blown the ears of the wheat. Does this matter? Not in the background where there is little or no definition, but the delicate nature of the ears of wheat in the foreground is spoiled by the wind. Or is it?

Perhaps you could see it in another way: do the blurred ears of corn represent the nature of a wheatfield in the wind better than an absolutely still picture would have done?

Film: Fujichrome 50 ASA
Camera: 6 x 6 centimetres
Lens: Telephoto
Exposure: 2 seconds at f.45
Filters: None

POINTS TO WATCH

● *Any intrusion into this picture would have upset its balance – a bit of another tree or the edge of the field would have ruined it.*
● *With an isolated tree, be sure never to cut into the shadow.*

EAST OF MERE, WILTSHIRE

A gain a logical sequence takes place in your mind. You want good colour saturation in the picture and to get that you have to use a slow film. Equally, you want to make sure that the poppies in the foreground and the trees in the distance are all completely sharp. You need in other words maximum depth of field. Such clarity from the back to the front of a photograph can only be achieved with a small aperture. And if the aperture is very small and the film speed is very low, the exposure time has to be long. You therefore need a very good tripod, a stable platform on which the camera can rest unmoving while the diaphragm is open.

If these steps are not followed the result would be blurred poppies and grass in the immediate foreground. Why would that be displeasing? Perhaps because you wouldn't know what it was. You don't want a red splodge where a poppy should be.

Film: Fujichrome 50 ASA
Camera: 6 x 6 centimetres
Lens: Wide angle
Exposure: 1/2 second at f.22
Filters: None

POINT TO WATCH

● *I should have pulled out the dandelions. and removed the white rocks leaning against the base of the tree in the middle distance on the right. Light coloured details distract.*

Allowing a Hint of Movement

KOKALA, SOUTH OF YITHIO, MANI, PELOPONNESE

You might imagine that this is a completely still scene, in which nothing ruffles the placidity of the landscape. But the long exposure has allowed a hint of movement to remain in the swirling of the water next to the beach. I don't think you would notice it if it were not pointed out, but it has had two important effects on the picture. The first is that there are no sharp edges to the breaking ripples as the wavelets approach the beach. The serenity of the distance and the absolute calm of the horizon are not interfered with by the any surface 'noise' in the foreground. And secondly, by allowing the water above the patches of green weed to swirl around for half a second, the area of green in the picture has been increased. Without those beautiful, and enlarged, patches of colour, the photograph would have been diminished.

Film: Fujichrome 50 ASA
Camera: 6 x 6 centimetres
Lens: Wide-angle
Exposure: 1/2 second at f.22
Filters: Polarising, 81c warm-up

POINTS TO WATCH

● *The stones underwater can only be seen because the polarising filter has taken reflections away. This is important because without the polarising filter it would have been much more difficult to see underwater in the foreground.*
● *The warm-up filter was not quite strong enough. The white stones on the beach are leaning towards the blue.*

The Presence of Time

Chesil Beach, Dorset

These two pictures are of exactly the same place and taken one after another. The only real variable is the length of time the film was exposed. The short exposure on this page has had various effects. The true colours of the beach, sea and sky have been registered by the film and the movement of the water has been stilled

In the foreground you will also notice that the shingle is out of focus. It was a very dark day and the film I had in the camera was a slow one (50 ASA). I needed to have a short exposure to still the water and so had to use a very wide aperture of f.5.6.

An aperture of f.11 would have been better for depth of field, but there was insufficient light and I had to compromise. I could of course have used a faster film but for the long exposure which I was planning to make next, that was the last thing I wanted. The slower the speed of the film, the easier it is to make a long exposure.

Film: Fujichrome 50 ASA
Camera: 6 x 6 centimetres
Lens: Wide-angle
Exposure: 1/30th second at f.5.6
Filter: Medium-density grey-graduated

CHESIL BEACH, DORSET

The long exposure above distorts colour and creates a strange and ghostly image as the surf washes back and forth across the shingle. It is in its way alluring if quite obviously unreal. This is the sort of effect which you might like to go for if you are thinking of setting a weird or romantic figure in the landscape. This is something I almost never do myself, but it is always good to know how to achieve an effect which you then might deliberately never use.

In order to reduce the amount of light coming on to the film two neutral density filters were sandwiched together in front of the lens, so that four times as much light was needed to expose the film as was needed in the first picture. Without them the frame would have been four stops over-exposed.

To add to the spooky effect, I have deliberately over-exposed the picture, using a 16-second exposure. If I had wanted to have the same density in the long-exposure photograph as in the one opposite, the settings would have been 8 seconds at f.22.

Film: Fujichrome 50 ASA
Camera: 6 x 6 centimetres
Lens: Wide angle
Exposure: 16 seconds at f.22
Filters: 2 two-stop neutral density (light-restricting)

POINTS TO WATCH

● *The 16-second exposure has altered the colour of the image. If you want to avoid this effect and maintain the natural colours, the film manufacturers always recommend appropriate filtration to prevent this when long exposures are made. Look at the instructions in the box of film.*

Manipulating the Image

The many kinds of filter and films of different speeds are all necessary tools of the trade. They represent the most manipulative side of landscape photography where it is not a question of responding to the landscape but of reshaping it according to your own aesthetic dictates. The chapter shows the ways in which they can be used and abused.

THIS BEECH AVENUE in Dorset in mid-winter, when all leaves have fallen and the beautiful grey of the trunks and long reaching arms of the trees, reveals itself as a thing almost more beautiful than when clothed in leaves. This photograph has manipulated the natural appearance of the avenue in two ways. I used very fast film to create a grainy effect and then softened that with a soft-focus filter. I hope that, if you didn't know to look for these effects, you wouldn't know that they were there. This, you would imagine, is simply a photograph which has about it an air of winter: rubbed down and cold. All that has been achieved by manipulating the image.

Most people think of fast film as useful in stopping movement. That is how sports photographers use it, but there is no reason why you shouldn't make use of it as I have done here for a static subject. Winter is never this colourless. It is the fast film, with its very low saturation, that has drained the colour out of the grass and bark.

And then there is the question of a soft-focus filter. It is something I use very rarely and it has acquired a very bad name through clumsy and exaggerated use. But I do think there is no need to be too precious about the use of photographic tools like these. To use a soft-focus filter does not necessarily mean that you have a gooey-eyed attitude to nature. It can be used, as I hope it is here, to reveal a beautiful if soft-edged aspect of the natural world.

NORTH OF WIMBORNE, DORSET

Film: Agfachrome 1000 ASA
Camera: 6 x 6 centimetres
Lens: Short telephoto
Exposure: 1/30 second at f. 22/32
Filter: Soft-focus

POINTS TO WATCH

● *The picture doesn't need any sky, because it is about the canopy of branches, the overfolding of trees and the relative lightlessness of a winter day. Never think that sky has to be in a landscape photograph. Only include something if it adds to the picture. Omit the redundant.*
● *Even in these conditions always try to get a good depth of field. Out of focus grain does not look the same as grain that has been softened by a filter.*

Enrich the Colours

KNOWLTON, DORSET

A polarising filter has two functions: it increases colour saturation across the whole picture, cutting out the white light reflecting from leaves, grass, walls and so on, allowing the true colour of the surface to shine through. It also has the effect of darkening a blue sky and as a result making the clouds more pronounced. It works at its most efficient when the sun is at right angles to the lens, i.e. to the right or left of you. When the sun is immediately ahead of or behind you, the polarising filter has little effect, simply because most of the light rays are coming straight at the camera.

This pair of photographs shows how very subtle indeed the effect of a polarising filter can be. The blue of the sky is slightly deepened, the clouds stand out a little more, the grass has a slightly richer colour, the textures of the rough bank in the foreground are lifted and as a result the whole picture

---

Film: Fujichrome 50 ASA
Camera: 6 x 6 centimetres
Lens: Wide angle
Exposure: 1/2 second at f.22
Filters: None

POINT TO WATCH

● *The sky here is a little bit messy, a fuss of clouds, neither one thing nor another. Another day might have been better, but in these conditions, where you have to pull out the stops, the polariser can give life to a picture which needs it.*

gains in substance and a sense of tangible reality. The polarising effect doesn't have to smack you between the eyes, although it often can. There are many occasions when it can make the blue of the sky too deep and sickly and this has to be guarded against. Where the sky becomes solid with colour it can completely overwhelm the landscape, which is never the required effect. For this reason, it is almost always a mistake to use a polariser when the sky is all blue. In those conditions consider half-polarising, turning the filter half a revolution, so that the sky acquires substance without garishness.

There is also another danger with a polariser which is difficult to avoid but almost never looks good in a photograph. The filter has a tendency to darken the corner of the sky which is furthest from the sun, but allows the sky to grow pale as it approaches the source of light. This is a recipe for imbalance and an unattractivce sky. You can sometimes adjust this, although it does not always work, by setting a medium-density grey-graduated filter over the corner of the frame which is nearest the sun.

Film: Fujichrome 50 ASA
Camera: 6 x 6 centimetres
Lens: Wide-angle
Exposure: 1 second at f.16/22
Filter: Polarising

POINTS TO WATCH

● *Remember the polarising filter cuts out a great deal of light, the very reflections whose purpose it is to remove. When using it, increase the exposure by 1 1/2 or 2 stops.*

● *Buildings do not look so good when the light is right behind the lens, because there are no shadows. Try to have the light striking the building obliquely.*

Warmth

HOLNEST, DORSET

Film: Fujichrome 50 ASA
Camera: 6 x 6 centimetres
Lens: Wide-angle
Exposure: 1/4 second at f.22
Filters: None

Film: Fujichrome 50 ASA
Camera: 6 x 6 centimetres
Lens: Wide-angle
Exposure: 1/4 second at f.22
Filter: 81a warm-up

The 81 series of light-balancing filters are useful for the way in which they can give an overall cast to a picture. The point of them is to turn the picture away from the blue end of the spectrum and towards the yellow. To put it more simply, they add warmth.

The effect of the series on a single scene is shown on these pages. Here in the first picture is an English country churchyard on a winter afternoon without any colour balancing filter in action. The frost is going too blue, especially in the shadows. It is difficult to register the differences between this and next picture, but if you flick your eye back and forth across these four pictures, you will see the effect of the 81 series. Something slightly off-putting or resistant in the unfiltered picture is almost invisibly removed. The blueness of the original image is 'cold' almost in an emotional sense. The fact that this is a photograph of a day which is physically cold makes an interesting point. The sense of physical cold is not diminished in the filtered photographs. It remains a frosty day throughout. But the photograph becomes more inviting, it becomes emotionally warmer.

Many photographers leave the 81a filter permanently on the lens as they prefer a warmer feel to their photographs. Its effect is slight but can be seen especially in the sky to the left of the church and in the light falling on the church walls themselves. It is a very subtle effect which you wouldn't notice if you didn't know the filter was there. It is almost as if you have added twenty minutes or so to the light of an evening. This might well be the source of its reality effect. You have no idea when this photograph was taken and the light cast by the filter is a perfectly likely sort of light to find late on a winter afternoon. The fact that it is 'untrue' matters far less than the feeling that it might be true.

There is an 81b warm-up filter but its effect is very similar to 81a and so we jump here to 81c. I think this is the most pleasing of all because its effect is quite definite but it is not trying to suggest a completely different light. It is just adding a touch of warmth, just about the right amount, so that the feeling is warm and friendly, the kind of place where you might like to find yourself.

The use of a filter will depend on what the light conditions are at the time. If the light is already very yellow then it may be that even an 81c may tip the scales of 'reality' just over the point of balance and you may have to make do with an 81a or 81b. It is, as ever, a question of remaining sensitive to the conditions at the time. Respond to what is happening.

Again, there is an 81d warm-up filter, which is halfway between 81c and 81ef. The effect of the ef is to give more of a sepia cast to the whole scene. It is quite noticeable in the finished product that you have altered the light to achieve an effect. I would not use this very often myself because it puts too conspicuous an overall cast on to the picture. Here, for example, the blue over most of the sky has been replaced by

something approaching yellow. The secret of good filter use is for the filter to be unnoticeable. And here the picture is certainly veering in the direction of an obvious effect. It is nothing like the way in which the 85 and 85b warm-up filters can reconstruct the scene (see overleaf) but this sepia colour is not quite what you would expect in a real scene. This is, however, a marginal question and in some circumstances the effect of an 81ef can be, as it needs to be, subliminal.

Film: Fujichrome 50 ASA
Camera: 6 x 6 centimetres
Lens: Wide-angle
Exposure: 1/4 second at f. 16/22
Filter: 81c warm-up

Film: Fujichrome 50 ASA
Camera: 6 x 6 centimetres
Lens: Wide-angle
Exposure: 1/4 second at f.16/22
Filter: 81ef warm-up

More Extreme Effects

HOLNEST, DORSET

The 85 warm-up steps outside the series in that it is not an amber filter so much as a pinky yellow one. The use of these filters is always subjective and I must confess I almost never like to give this extra pinky feel to a landscape. I do not think it works particularly well here, for example, because to me it looks false, the colour cast extreme, so that there is a rather sugary sweet air to it, as if the picture had been

Film: Fujichrome 50 ASA
Camera: 6 x 6 centimetres
Lens: Wide-angle
Exposure: 1/2 second at f.22
Filter: 85 warm-up

coated with a strawberry flavoured sauce. That can't be suitable to an English church-yard in winter. It is too coy for words.

The distinction between the 85b and the

81 series is that the 85b is very distinctly a sepia filter, rather than the plain ambers of the 81 series. This picture involves another confession. The 85b sums up everything in a sort of photography that I most dislike. Its caramel coating is widely used in commercial photography to give a theatrical, enriched, evening feel to a picture. But the effect somehow manages to be both exaggerated and trivial at the same time, visibly false and in no way respectful of the tone or meanings of a place. I never use it myself because it seems to me too easy and too careless a way of treating a landscape. The picture says 'Here I am, a filter in an English churchyard.' And can that be the point of landscape photography? It blurs distinctions, it places something between you and the landscape rather than revealing the nature of the place itself, it imposes the sentimental warmth of a certain vision of landscape which involves a kind of blindness to its realities. You have no need to leave home to get this kind of effect. It might as well be a photograph of the latest brown bread advertisement you have seen on TV.

POINT TO WATCH

● *The real purpose of the 85b is when you have a tungsten balance film in your camera and you want to photograph in daylight. You must convert the daylight into the sort of light produced by artificial tungsten bulbs and that is what the 85b can do. Conversely an 80a colour-correction filter, which is blue, must be used when daylight balanced film is used under tungsten light. The light from a flash is equivalent to daylight.*

Film: Fujichrome 50 ASA
Camera: 6 x 6 centimetres
Lens: Wide-angle
Exposure: 1/2 second at f.22
Filter: 85b warm-up

Time of Day

GUADALEST, NEAR MALAGA, ANDALUCIA

The bright geometrical elements of this hill-village in southern Spain were being cut by a sharp morning light. This first picture is almost as it appeared to the eye. Only a polarising filter has been used to deepen the richness of the sky and to bring out the beautiful wispiness of the clouds, as an effective contrast with the hard-edged shapes of the village below them.

But there is something too hard and too blue about the whites in this picture. They need the warmth of evening light to convey the full romance of a village in southern Spain.

> Film: Fujichrome 50 ASA
> Camera: 6 x 6 centimetres
> Lens: Wide-angle
> Exposure: 1/4 second at f. 22
> Filter: Polarising, fully polarised

POINTS TO WATCH

● *Use a polarising filter to take the glare off the roofs and add richness to tiles and sky.*
● *Mid-morning light, in which the blue element is dominant, tends to make whites harsh and unreceptive.*
● *Beware: polarising filters will increase the contrast in photograhs, and tend to take detail out of the shadows*

You might think – I hope you think! – that I returned to the same spot the same evening and took this second picture. It is soaked in the yellow warmth of the end of the day. The blue harshness of morning has gone. Now there is something of the dreamy air of warm evening. All this is achieved with the use of a filter; the photograph was, in fact, taken a few minutes after the one on the left.

To my mind, subtlety and mildness are the key to the successful use of filters. The picture is already a failure if someone asks 'I wonder what filter he used?' A good photograph should be like a good dinner; one shouldn't be tempted to say 'I wonder how on earth the chef managed that!', but simply 'What a delicious thing this is...'

> Film: Fujichrome 50 ASA
> Camera: 6 x 6 centimetres
> Lens: Wide-angle
> Exposure: 1/4 second at f. 16 / f. 22
> Filters: Polarising, fully polarised
> 81c warm-up

POINTS TO WATCH

● *Any filter denser than 81c(used here) would create a tangerine effect that would look artificial.*
● *Beware: green foliage under warm-up filters tends to turn yellowy-brown.*

In fact, I did go back in the evening, to a slightly different vantage-point. The last rays of the sun are now coming from the right, just clipping one or two of the houses. No filters of any kind have been used here and the softness of the light is quite natural.

Film: Fujichrome 50 ASA
Camera: 6 x 6 centimetres
Lens: Wide-angle
Exposure: 1 second at f. 22
Filters: None

POINTS TO WATCH

● *Using the real qualities of the light will always produce a better image than manipulating it with filters.*
● *Wait for the reflected light of evening, with its low contrast, to achieve a warm and soft effect.*
● *Low, shadowless light allows you to achieve an even colour saturation over the whole picture. In lighting of higher contrast, the actual density of colour in the picture will vary. The effect of that will be to produce a less tranquil and more visually dynamic picture.*

The Play of Light

Use light to enhance the drama of a picture, setting the light against the dark, catching the first and the last of the light, manoeuvring the lit object aginst an unlit background. Very low light or the light in a rainstorm can bring more to a picture than bright sunshine, which often flattens or dilutes a subject. As ever, wait for conditions to come right.

A PHOTOGRAPHER has to know, care, think and learn about light as a sculptor must come to understand stone. Light is the medium, an intangible, frustrating and utterly astonishing substance, inside which the photographer has to work.

It is never still and your only task is to wait until the light begins to do for you what you hope it might. Visualise the picture as you would like it to be, which parts lit, which in shadow, and wait, almost literally, for your dreams to come true. There is no other way to go about it. Your only control over the play of light is to capture it at the moment it suits you best.

This afternoon in the Cévennes, the sky was immensely dark and heavy, with a small blue hole in it miles away to the right. The sky was moving as a body. Often in these cases the hole closes up and the moment for which you have been waiting disappears. Or the spotlight misses the place on which you want it to shine. Twenty feet here or there would make all the difference. On this afternoon I waited two hours. A wind shift would have killed it. But it arrived and caught the château where I wanted it. I took four frames in the space of 30 seconds and then it was gone, the spotlight shut off, the château returned to the dark.

That was a lucky moment. I have had many occasions when the light slid off sideways and the waiting turned out to be pointless, or at least pictureless: waiting will always allow your understanding of the place to grow.

NEAR FLORAC, LOZERE

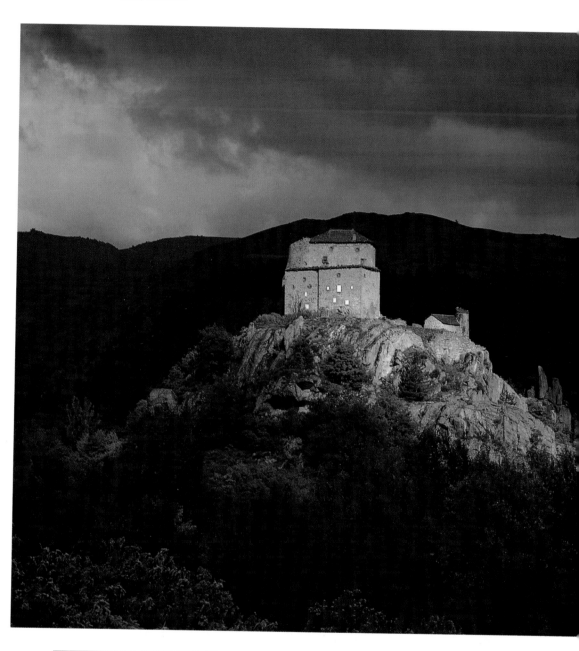

Film: Fujichrome 50 ASA
Camera: 6 x 6 centimetres
Lens: Short telephoto
Exposure: 1 second at f.32
Filters: 81b warm-up

POINTS TO WATCH

● *In a spotlit landscape expose only for the lit areas. A general exposure will reveal detail in parts of the frame where you do not particularly want it.*

● *Midday light would have looked too blue. An 81b warm-up filter kills the blue tinge and adds warmth to the scene.*

● *Don't compromise or give up. This is worth waiting for. A photograph of the château in a different light might have looked like a postcard.*

The Layering of Light

MARSHWOOD VALE, DORSET

The layering of light is a depth-creating effect that is often used in the theatre. It can walk you right back into a picture. Here the effect is produced by the last light as it catches the ridges in Marshwood Vale in southern Dorset. The result is that you can survey the whole scene displayed in front of you.

The layers of light help the eye; they are a demonstration of depth. Imagine the valley without them. Distance would still be there but it would be a distance that was neither interesting nor beautiful. The effect here is not created by light alone: the sheep are an indispensable aid to this creation of depth; their diminishing scale is quite literally a key to distance.

Film: Ektachrome 64 ASA
Camera: 6 x 6 centimetres
Lens: Wide-angle
Exposure: 1/8 second at f.22
Filters: Polarising, fully polarised

POINTS TO WATCH

● *Be careful not to cut animals in half. It is as great a sin as cutting the head off a person in a portrait.*
● *The long exposure has blurred the animals on the far left and in the mid-distance. This could have been avoided by using a faster film, which would have needed a shorter exposure. But that would have involved a loss of definition as fast film will always produce a grainy image. This choice must lie with the individual.*

However often I look at this photograph of the eroded, seaweedy rocks at the mouth of the River Erme on the South Devon coast, it never loses its air of unreality – or at least its atmosphere of strange half-reality. I am not quite sure what lies behind this effect, but it is something to do with the way in which the theatrical lighting, seen in the previous picture, is doubled here: a well lit sandy apron is backed by the dark flat of the rocks; behind them again the rear of the stage is brightly lit (from a hidden light-source). The dark cloudy sky acts as the rear wall of the theatre.

ERME MOUTH, SOUTH DEVON

Film: Ektachrome 64 ASA
Camera: 6 x 6 centimetres
Lens: Wide-angle
Exposure: 1/4 second at f.22
Filters: Polarising, fully polarised

POINT TO WATCH

● *You may be able to detect places where I had walked about on the sand when trying to find the photograph here. I have tried to cover up my footprints by brushing the sand, but this is a good lesson: don't be careless about where you walk. You may be ruining the picture you have not yet noticed.*

Splashes of Light

BUTTERMERE, CUMBRIA

The splashed and lovely light in this photograph has always seemed to me beautiful for the reason that its effect seems particularly unforced. The sun is just out of the top corner of the frame and the trees are luminous from the backlighting which this gives them. There is always a danger with backlighting that light will fall directly on the lens and flare – to my mind an ugly and disruptive presence in any picture – will result. The best way of avoiding that, as I have managed to do here, is to find a patch of shade which falls directly on to the camera.

The generous feeling in the picture, as though light and shade in equal quantities have been liberally doled out all over it, comes from that rounded, almost unordered patterning of the light.

But there are other effects here too. The hillside in the background, which is in total shade, has a soft, velvety feel to it – it is lit only by light reflected off the sky and other parts of the landscape. And that movement – from the shade in which the camera stands, through the splashes of light, to the profound calm of the distant shadow is, I think, one of the reasons this photograph strikes one as beautiful.

Film: Ektachrome 64 ASA
Camera: 6 x 6 centimetres
Lens: Wide-angle
Exposure: 1/8 second at f.16/f.22
Filters: Polarising, low densitygrey graduated

POINTS TO WATCH

● *The use of a low-density grey graduated filter is necessary here to bring the brightness of the sky within the exposure range of the film. Be careful, in a picture with such a high horizion, that the dark part of the filter does not clip the tops of the hills and the tips of the trees on the left.*

● *The exposure on a windy day needs to be 1/8 second or faster to still the movement of water and trees.*

The Lit Foreground

NEAR CASTELLANE, ALPES DE HAUTE PROVENCE

Imagine for a moment that the lighting conditions in this picture are reversed, with a light mountain and a dark foreground. The whole meaning of the image shifts because, obviously enough, light emphasises and shadow diminishes. That would have been a picture of a mountain led up to by a valley. What you have in fact is a valley overlooked by a mountain.

The light, which is low and late, is apparently sourceless but I am not entirely happy with the effect in this picture. The light on the clump of trees near the left-hand edge should not be there, nor on the great expanse of rather uninteresting grass. Better would have been a concentrated beam concentrating only on the central clump of trees.

If that had been the case, and it is in fact not far from it, there would have been a very satisfying symmetry between the lit and the dark parts of the photograph.

Film: Fujichrome 50 ASA
Camera: 6 x 6 centimetres
Lens: Wide-angle
Exposure: 1 second at f.22
Filters: None

POINT TO WATCH

● *Try putting your hand across the bottom of the picture, cutting out most of the grass. I think that improves the picture; the confrontation of hill and valley, lit and dark, is more concentrated.*

A dramatic set needs dramatic lighting and there are few places in Europe more astonishing, at least in terms of the way a building sits in the landscape, than the monasteries at Meteora. It is absolutely necessary that the monastery itself is lit. This picture was taken early in the morning and the lighting conditions are almost perfect for the subject.

Every light patch is set against a dark one. A farm in a field might demand flat light, but a monastery on a pinnacle cannot need anything but a series of highlights set against shadows.

Later in the day would not have worked. As the the sun rose, light was getting into those shadows in the rock clefts and within a few minutes one would have ended up with a pale monastery against a pale background. There would have been no picture at all.

Film: Fujichrome 50 ASA
Camera: 6 x 6 centimetres
Lens: Short telephoto
Exposure: 1/2 second at f.32
Filter: Polarising, fully polarised

POINTS TO WATCH

● *The sky is weak. Even a mild grey graduated filter would have affected the tops of the rock stacks and looked messy.*

● *No matter how many ultra-violet filters you put on the front of the lens, you can only cut down a certain amount of blue haze. It would certainly have grown worse during the day.*

METEORA, THESSALIA

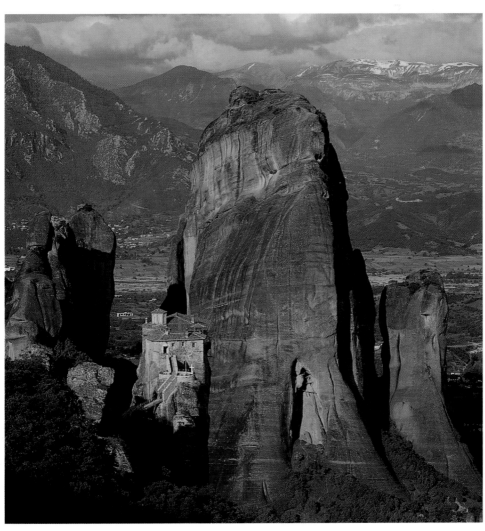

Where Light Confirms the Nature of the Place

EAST OF RONCAL, NAVARRA

This was very late in the day and the shadows were racing up the poplars. The sun was sitting on the top edge of the cliff behind. At first sight, I knew that these were the light conditions that could confirm the nature of the place. A massive wall of rock, steely blue and calm in the shadow, patterned with beautiful ox-bow curves where it had been shaped underground in ancient movements of the mountains.

And in front of that the glittering, backlit, visually mobile poplars. One can almost hear them rustling. It is a scene of opposites, perfectly folded in with each other, and which any other light conditions would certainly have diminished.

Film: Fujichrome 50 ASA
Camera: 6 x 6 centimetres
Lens: Short telephoto
Exposure: 1/4 second at f.22/f.32
Filters: None

POINTS TO WATCH

● *It is important not to use a polarising filter if you want to keep the sparkle on the leaves.*
● *Try to get animals as neat as they are here, all pointing in the same direction.*
● *The short telephoto lens brings the picture tight in on its subject, but in doing so limits your room for manoeuvre. You have to make the picture on the spot, and not take a wider frame and later pull the picture you want out of it.*

DURNESS, SUTHERLAND

It is rarely clear at the time why a photograph seems to work, why the vision in the view-finder is a pleasing thing, but it is possible to analyse it afterwards. There are several elements at work in this photograph of a reservoir in Sutherland: the complete stillness of the water; the beautiful and sharply distinct colours of hill, heather, pebble and sky; the framing of the distant mountain by the reservoir banks. But none of this would mean as much as it does without the specific qualities of the evening light. This is almost the last moment of the lit day and I had waited here three hours for it.

Because I have framed the photograph so that the horizon comes almost three-quarters of the way up the picture, the part of the sky reflected in the water in the foreground is different from the part of the sky seen in the distance. It so happened, on this evening, that the sky was intensely black overhead and lighter, more grey, in the distance. The result, which doubles and enriches the presence of the sky in the photograph, establishes bands of light and dark in the picture. That is picked up in the foreground where a beam of late evening light is clipping the pebbles on the shore, so that their brightness is set against the blackest part of the reflected sky. The picture arranges itself through these successive layers of light and dark.

Film: Ektachrome 64 ASA
Camera: 6 x 6 centimetres
Lens: Wide-angle
Exposure: 1 second at f.22
Filter: Low density grey graduated

Calm

SAN GIMIGNANO, TUSCANY

If I was going to design an ideal landscape, this is the sort of place I would end up with. It is stable, structured, varied and complete. There is immediate order in the vineyard and an air of aesthetic coherence in the almost perfectly round coppice in the heart of the valley. Nothing conceals anything else. The land clearly belongs to the city and the city crowns the land, its visible head. This is surely a picture of the pastoral dream of what life might be like in the ideal state. But it is not embalmed. The smoke drifting from the bonfire is a crucially mobile element in the picture.

And for this dream of a possible reality, a place without anxiety, the light is calm, flat and diffuse, neither dramatic nor harsh.

Film: Fujichrome 50 ASA
Camera: 6 x 6 centimetres
Lens: Standard
Exposure: 1/4 second at f.22
Filters: 81b warm-up

POINTS TO WATCH

● *I would have preferred the central vine to be in the very middle of the picture to get some sort of linear perfection, but there was a large red oil drum just out of the frame to the right which forced this slight asymmetry.*
● *The 81b warm-up filter has done a great deal to bring out the yellow that would otherwise merely lurk within the vine leaves.*

Magnificence

St Claude Valfin, Jura

Only very rarely does a photograph continue to give me as much pleasure as this one. I feel nothing but gratitude for finding this place on the day and at the time of year that I did. Some rules had to go by the board – the bases of many of the trees have been cut off, but there is no problem with that because the rest of the photograph sweeps you up with the completeness of it. Sky and land are in unison, both in tone and shape. The pattern of scattered yellow larches diminishes towards a distance that holds a small bowl of mist in the valley.

But I think there is something at work in this picture which is not immediately apparent and may be the reason why I continue to like it so much. It is, in a way, a sleight of hand. The brightness of the yellow trees leads one to think that they are brightly lit. Usually that sort of intensity of colour only comes from something on which the sun is shining directly, or even when they are backlit and you are actually seeing the light of the sun through them.

But those are not the light conditions here at all. The light is actually as flat and diffused as in the photograph of San Gimignano on the previous page. So the effect, in one photograph, is full of two contradictory things: calm and excitement, flat light and sharp light, drama and ease. This, I think, must be the source of the pleasure this picture gives me, and perhaps it is a rule than could be generalised. If you have magnificent colour in a landscape, try to photograph it in as flat a light as you can.

Film: Ektachrome 64 ASA
Camera: 6 x 6 centimetres
Lens: Wide-angle
Exposure: 1/2 second at f.22
Filters: 81b warm-up, low density grey graduated

POINTS TO WATCH

● *Without the 81b warm-up filter the sky would have been greyish. It needs some warmth to relate it to what is going on down below.*
● *The graduated filter brings out the mottling in the cloud, to give it a sense of structure.*

Choosing the Moment

EAST OF ILLORA, ANDALUCIA

As a band of sunlight moves across a scene, you have before you the choice of where to place it in the landscape. These two photographs were taken a few moments apart. In the picture above, the face of the house is too similar to the tone of the earth behind it. There is not enough contrast between them and so definition is lost and drama reduced.

You might imagine that it is light which carries information but that is not strictly

Film: Fujichrome 50 ASA
Camera: 6 x 6 centimetres
Lens: Telephoto
Exposure: 2 seconds at f.45
Filters: None

true. It is the distinction between light and dark that conveys meaning, and here that distinction is not clear enough. On those grounds it is quite clear that the picture on the opposite page works better.

EAST OF ILLORA, ANDALUCIA

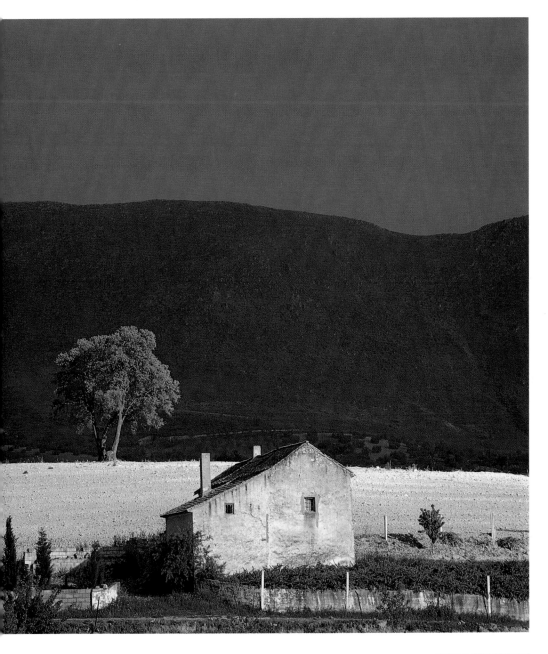

But that is not the end of the story. Try blocking out the sky with your hand on the picture above. The large bright patch of the sky is removed and a chance is given to the house. Now try removing the sky from the picture on the opposite page. For some reason, that picture then dies on you. Why? It is to do with the way in which the placing of light distributes weight around a picture and the sense of balance which the eye intuitively demands. But this experiment

Film: Fujichrome 50 ASA
Camera: 6 x 6 centimetres
Lens: Telephoto
Exposure: 2 seconds at f.45
Filters: None

does make one thing clear. Always take more than one frame when you have shifting and dramatic light conditions, simply to cover opportunities which you might not have recognised at the time.

Colour in its Place

Colour, in all its forms, is one of the greatest pleasures of photography, from blaring garishness to the suppressed, near-monochrome of a winter landscape. The chapter discusses the many uses of colour: the creation of a visual concordance, the isolation of a single colour element and allowing a landscape a full and varied palette.

IF YOU DO FIND a colour that screams at you, make an issue of it. One of the drawbacks of colour photography is that things can be too colourful. But sometimes the only option is to make the lurid even more lurid, to abandon good taste and allow what is, after all, there to shout at you.

But with such loud colour there is one overriding rule: do not make the structure too fussy. These pictures work by denying subtlety, slamming on the colour and amazing by their sheer chromatic presence. There is nothing to read between the lines because nothing is concealed. It is this almost nursery-style simplicity of colour, coming in large, identifiable blocks, that, for this sort of picture, you must look for. A straight-forward idea: loud must be simple.

It is worth asking whether this picture would have worked without the shed and trees. Perhaps it would but at a slightly lower level. I don't think I was aware of it at the time, but everything in the picture I have arranged as tightly as possible. Those structural elements are the means by which the photograph is screwed down tight. The two trees are exactly symmetrical about the shed. And the shed is bang in the middle of the frame. This has meant that I have not been able to look straight along the lines of the lavender, but that is unimportant. It is worth noticing just how hideous a building this asbestos-roofed, breeze-block shed is. Another simple lesson: very strong colour can override what might have been the drawbacks in the photograph.

NEAR VAISON-LA-ROMAINE, PROVENCE

Film: Fujichrome 50 ASA
Camera: 6 x 6 centimetres
Lens: Short telephoto
Exposure: 1/4 second at f.22/f.32
Filter: Polarising, fully polarised

POINTS TO WATCH

● *The polarising filter by cutting out reflected light saturates the film with colour. This adds enormously to the uncompromising effect needed here. Reflections would have lessened the colour density and you would have started to pay more attention to the (fairly unattractive) appearance of the shed.*

● *Notice how the highlight at the the end of the shed shapes the picture. Use your finger to block it out and see how much the photograph loses.*

The Complementary and the Different

NORTH OF MONTEVARCHI, TUSCANY

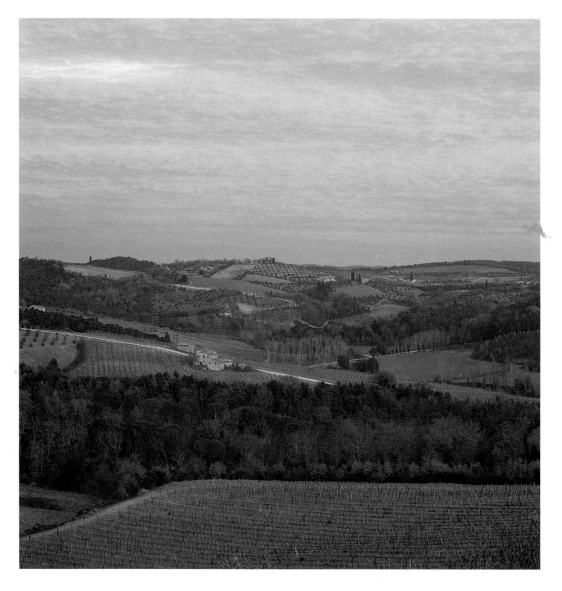

This winter landscape is fast asleep, hibernating. The sun had set at least half an hour before this picture was taken. The sky alone is lit by the sun. There is no direct light on the land, and so the two elements of the landscape are seen in different conditions. There is something unsettling about that. No one would ever have chosen this combination of colours for their clothes. Some kind of silky grey would have been the sky colour that fitted. But this is a picture that works by bringing two uncomplementary things up against each other.

Film: Fujichrome 50 ASA
Camera: 6 x 6 centimetres
Lens: Short telephoto
Exposure: 2 seconds at f.32
Filters: None

POINT TO WATCH

● *Do always – and this is something one can only repeat – check around the edges of the frame of the photograph. Nothing extraneous should be there. Here, in an ideal world, the olive branches at the bottom and at the bottom right would have been excluded.*

This is the other side of the coin. Here everything is soaked in the same liquid colour of the evening: orange leaves, tiles, light. The mild warm-up filter I used did little to enhance the natural and astonishing terracotta of the air, the last light scattered by the dust at the end of a hot day. It is like a musical chord in which each of the surfaces in the landscape – the ochreish patina on the walls, the lichened ochre of the tiles – makes its own separate but concordant note. If you want this effect, look for the place whose own natural colours match the colour of the light you expect to find.

BONNIEUX, NEAR APT, VAUCLUSE

Film: Fujichrome 50 ASA
Camera: 6 x 6 centimetres
Lens: Short telephoto
Exposure: 2 seconds at f.32
Filter: 81b warm-up

POINTS TO WATCH

● *The very low light has meant a long two-second expoure. Anything with any movement in it will blur in that length of time, but for this sort of picture, that does not matter enormously. The point here is mood and suggestiveness, not precision.*
● *Use a warm-up filter to enhance natural light.*

A Moment of Colour

South of Oyarzun, Guipuzcoa, Cantabria

Here is something quite familiar from another context but enacted in a different way: the single statement, not here in terms of form but purely in terms of colour. You must be very careful if you are going to try this: the shape of the colour block itself is crucial – it must be a beautiful thing; the colour relationships between the central revealed object and the colours and shapes surrounding it are equally important.

I am pleased with this picture, with the mouth shape and the beautiful milky green of the dew-soaked grass of the field, the placing of the haystacks, the russet of the surrounding hills. It is like a slash in a cloth, a revelation of the colour of the flesh underneath.

Film: Fujichrome 50 ASA
Camera: 6 x 6 centimetres
Lens: Telephoto
Exposure: 2 seconds at f.45
Filter: Polarising

POINTS TO WATCH

● *Don't let the excitement of the main focus of the picture allow you to forget the outer edges, which if uncontrolled distract from the central idea. Another splash of green, for example, would have totally undermined the picture.*
● *On this overcast day there are no highlights. But that is fine; the colour itself, rather than the patterning of light and shade, organises the structure of the picture.*

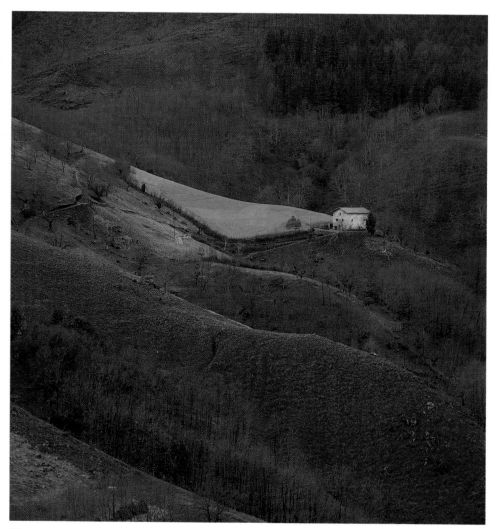

I was looking due west as the sun sank under the horizon. Anything photographed into a bright light will appear in silhouette, but the two silhouettes here have taken on quite different and beautifully concordant colours. The mauve of the mountains is perhaps influenced by the the mist rising from the swamp that lay between them and me. The trees are in fact utterly black but a strange trick of the eye makes them appear orange. But the point is this: the control of structure in a fully coloured photograph is quite crucial. If the colour is this dramatic, keep the form strict and simple.

Film: Fujichrome 50 ASA
Camera: 6 x 6 centimetres
Lens: Wide-angle
Exposure: 1 second at f.22
Filter: 81b warm-up

POINT TO WATCH

● *Fractional movement in the water over the long one-second exposure necessary in these light conditions hazes the reflection of the trees slightly. This is both unavoidable and beautiful in itself. It is another example of that familiar recipe: the repetition of something, but with a slight difference.*

NEAR SELESTAT, SOUTH OF STRASBOURG, BAS-RHIN

Black and White Colour

CHARLESTOWN, CORNWALL

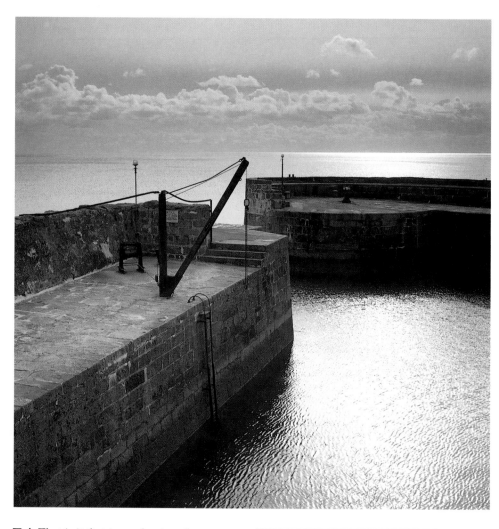

What is it that is so pleasing about an almost colourless colour photograph? I think it might be, at least in part, the sight of something operating so utterly within its capabilities. Here is modern colour film, able to reproduce so much that is so ferociously chromatic, being used to reproduce the nearly monochrome. It is similar to the phenomenon of a Rolls Royce cruising downhill at no more than ten miles an hour.

But there is also something more: the pleasure of the simple rarity. A scene as drained of colour as this is as uncommon in the natural landscape as something which is as bright with colour as the lavender field on page 95.

Film: Ektachrome 64 ASA
Camera: 6 x 6 centimetres
Lens: Wide-angle
Exposure: 1/8 second at f.22
Filter: High density grey graduated

POINTS TO WATCH

● *This is a very heavily backlit scene . The sky was very bright; to bring it within the tonal range which the film could deal with, I had to use a heavy grey graduated filter. The detail in the cloud here was not visible to the naked eye.*

● *You can always use a graduated filter at the coast. The absolute flatness of a sea horizon means there is no danger of the dark part of the filter invading parts of the picture, such as a hill or a tree, where it would have been unwelcome.*

I love these khaki grey beiges. It is as if someone has a put a single drop of colour into a glass of water and then washed the whole landscape with the mixture, the subtlest and slightest of colour gestures. Even in the warming light of late afternoon, even with the polarising filter on to squeeze out what colour was there, this remains a mute, understated, cool denial of everything you might expect to find in an Italian landscape. And that, I think, is the key. Removing colour allows you to stand outside the over-colourful, postcard way of seeing things. It is a way of saying 'Look: this is something that was there but which you did not bother to see.'

Film: Fujichrome 50 ASA
Camera: 6 x 6 centimetres
Lens: Standard
Exposure: 1 second at f.22
Filters: Polarising, half polarised,
low density grey graduated

POINTS TO WATCH

● *Winter is the time for delineated shapes and reduced colour. The greenery of summer is a thickening thing which tends to obliterate form. Where summer is fleshy, winter is bony. It is often the time when you can get a new look at the over-familiar.*

● *Use a polarising filter to squeeze the last remaining drops of colour from the day.*

WEST OF SINALUNGA, TUSCANY

Something Over Which the Eye Can Roam

SAN MINIATO, SOUTH OF FLORENCE, TUSCANY

In the end, there is something about distortions of colour in the landscape – either exaggerating it, or over-selecting it or almost removing it – which does not treat the landscape with the respect and subtlety it deserves. And there is something else about a photograph like this one in Tuscany which in its suggestive, detailed, easy, undemonstrative, accommodating beauty goes beyond those more obvious manipulations. Here is something over which the eye can roam – delicately orchestrated by the slight formal gesture made by the two trees, but going beyond that to a composition of colour and form which embraces an entire constellation of feelings and memories of Italy, something for which no formula, no tried and trusted way of doing things, can really prepare you.

Film: Fujichrome 50 ASA
Camera: 6 x 6 centimetres
Lens: Short telephoto
Exposure: 1 second at f.32
Filters: None

POINT TO WATCH

● *Consider for as long as you can before deciding what picture to take in a place. Stay with it so that the photograph might include the less obvious meanings to be found there. Here the two trees were the first thing that caught my eye, but I realised after a while that they were only part of something bigger, better, richer, softer and more long-lasting. Familiarity can often breed content.*

Sky and the Landscape

The sky is the most mobile element within any landscape and the source of a great deal of its drama. This chapter shows how to make the sky fit in with the landscape below it and, both in the daytime and in the dramatics of a sunset, how to use it to establish an element in the picture which the landscape itself cannot provide.

WHEN THESE ROUND straw bales first began to appear in English fields – it was in the late 1970s – I immediately took to them, for their lovely big shapes, their big sculptural gestures in the landscape. On the face of it, they look easy enough to make a picture of, but it is harder than you would think. Getting them in position, getting them into a pattern that satisfies, I have often found infuriatingly difficult. But this picture was different. I saw the bales of straw and, at almost the same time, in the distance, the rolls of cumulus approaching from the west. It was extraordinary – a bank of cloud rolling towards what seemed like its (photographic) destiny. I simply waited and clicked as the moment happened, and the patterns coincided.

This was obviously an extraordinary and rare occasion when the shapes of the clouds exactly and precisely matched the shapes on the landscape below them. That sort of thing does not happen every day. But the principle, if in a more muted form, remains the same: that you should establish a relationship between sky and earth.

The heart of a good sky in a photograph, I think, consists in your conceiving what is front of you not in terms of two elements which have to be brought into relationship with each other, but as a pair. One part is in motion and the other is still but reflects the changes going on overhead. Think of sky and earth as an indissoluble coupling and you will not go far wrong.

NEAR STONEHENGE, WILTSHIRE

Film: Ektachrome 64 ASA
Camera: 6 x 6 centimetres
Lens: Wide-angle
Exposure: 1/2 second at f.22
Filters: Polarising

POINTS TO WATCH

● *If symmetry suggests itself in sky and landscape, do your best to make use of it.*
● *Make sure that the gaps between repeated single objects such as these bales remain clear.*
● *Here the sun was directly behind me. In this situation you should be careful that neither your own shadow nor the shadow of the camera on the tripod appears in the photograph. Here, I am afraid, the camera shadow has crept in. A pity, but not, I hope, noticeable unless pointed out.*

The Sympathetic Sky

Mont Sainte Victoire, Bouches-du-Rhone

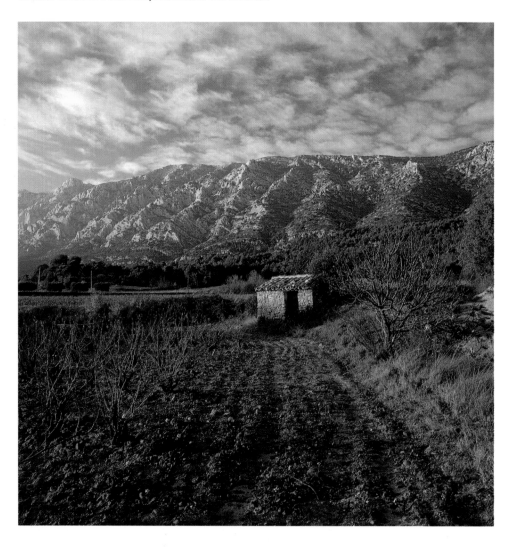

If you half shut your eyes and look at this picture of Mont Sainte Victoire, what do you see?

A single textured, bobbled cloth in three rough, almost woollen stripes, the colour of the red earth, of the mountain and of the sky? I hope so because of all the pictures I have taken, this is the one that most conveys that magical *continuousness* of tone between sky and earth and everything that grows on it. This is something that can often be felt when you are in a beautiful place but which a photograph can only rarely convey. It is a point where for once the sky is sympathetic to the flecky, speckled, flickering surface of the earth.

Film: Ektachrome 64 ASA
Camera: 6 x 6 centimetres
Lens: Wide-angle
Exposure: 1/2 second at f.22
Filters: Polarising

POINTS TO WATCH

● *Don't allow one element to dominate.*
To preserve the coherence of a picture like this all parts must be in balance. A heavy graduated filter would have overcooked the sky.

● *This picture would not have worked without the low light revealing the grittiness of the soil or creating the shadow in the mountains. When I passed this place again, several years later, and the light was different, I hardly recognised it.*

The long exposure on the water has silkened it, bringing it up to the texture of the sky, so that the water looks to me like beaten copper, the hammer marks still on it. A shorter exposure would have toughened up that surface, giving far more defined edges to the reflections. But that would have been wrong, disrupting the concurrence that is now there in the picture. But it is colour as well as texture that comes together here – in the water and in the roofs and walls of the town. The sky was in fact grey and I have brought it into line with the other colours of the picture by using a graduated filter. So this, in the end, via filters and long exposures, is something of a manipulated image, achieving artificially an effect something like what was there naturally at Mont Sainte Victoire.

Film: Ektachrome 64 ASA
Camera: 6 x 6 centimetres
Lens: Wide-angle
Exposure: 1 second at f.22
Filters: Low density grey graduated

POINT TO WATCH

● *When photographing sun reflected in water, watch out for unwanted and disruptive flare in the lens. With water, there are always two suns to look out for.*

CANDES SAINT MARTIN, LOIRE

The Sheltering Sky

THE MANGER, UFFINGTON, BERKSHIRE

The soft and female shapes and colours of the chalk landscape of southern England reach their most perfect form in this combe near Uffington in Berkshire. The land is fleshy and animal in shape and feel, a huge body laid out on a sofa, rolls of flesh, or the eight fat fingers of a millionaire's hand clustered around the stub of a cigar. And in this, the black sky plays an all-important role: it *disciplines* the picture, holding it in, so that the viewer's attention doesn't wander off into the uninteresting distance. The natural light makes the drama clear: lit flesh against a dark background.

Film: Ektachrome 64 ASA
Camera: 6 x 6 centimetres
Lens: Wide-angle
Exposure: 1/4 second at f.22
Filters: Medium density grey graduated

POINTS TO WATCH

● *The razor edge of light along the ridge on the left hand side is important to the shapeliness of the photograph – to the revelation of shape within the picture. Block it out or imagine it away and see how the picture is diminished.*

● *A high viewpoint like this – level with the clouds – almost always adds to a picture. It helps to box in what is interesting in the landscape.*

This place could have made a very good photograph. These strange tree stumps, half-drowned, immediately struck me as very odd looking things, creatures from space or giant fossilised starfish. But this was an utterly wasted opportunity. It could have been so much better than what I ended up with here. The sky is the mess. It is too obviously artificial and has no real identity or character. That blue splurge at the top of the frame comes simply from a massive overuse of the polarising filter. One simple lesson emerges. You can enhance but you cannot add. I have tried here to give the sky a depth and resonance that was never there and the picture should not have been taken.

Film: Ektachrome 64 ASA
Camera: 6 x 6 centimetres
Lens: Wide-angle
Exposure: 1/4 second at f.22
Filters: Polarising

POINT TO WATCH

● *Don't think a polarising filter will make a picture whatever the conditions.*

ALEMOOR LOCH, HAWICK, BORDERS

The Sky's Great Finale

NAFPLION, PELOPONNESE

I almost never photograph a sunset. But there is no need to be frightened of the beauty in something which everybody considers beautiful. Searching for the unusual or the hidden beauty is all right if it stops short of becoming a rule or a fetish. Why not take a sunset for what it can give you now and then? It is, of course, not good enough simply to pick up the camera and point it at a red sky. You must first wait until almost the very last moment, when the sun has nearly gone. Otherwise you will get flare in the lens. Even then you must use a graduated filter to darken the sun – it is always much brighter than you think – and to bring the brightness range within the limits that the film can deal with. In this case it was important to have detail both in sky and sea. Without the graduated filter and at this length of exposure, the sky would have appeared totally burnt out. If I had exposed for the sky without the filter (which would have been a much shorter exposure) the sea would have appeared almost completely black and without detail.

> Film: Fujichrome 50 ASA
> Camera: 6 x 6 centimetres
> Lens: Wide-angle
> Exposure: 1 second at f.22
> Filters: 81c warm-up, medium
> density grey graduated

POINT TO WATCH

● *A sunset is the sky's great finale to the day. This is the moment when the sky takes centre stage and to give it what it deserves, you must lower the horizon as I have done here. This is especially true over broken water, where the sky is rich with information but the water contains very little indeed.*

Water and the Landscape

Water is the most magical and alluring of all elements in the landscape, particularly for the many and varied ways it relates to light in a landscape. Look for the differences between still and moving water, for its combinations of reflective and translucent qualities and the different ways that water can convey a mood.

The trees in this picture take up only about 1/40th of the picture space. Nevertheless they manage to dominate the scene. Why? Partly, I think, because they are are placed so squarely in the middle of the frame, commanding the scene like an actor performing a soliloquy. But the reflecting water plays a key part too, as if, to continue the analogy, it were the audience, reflecting the importance of what is happening on stage.

I am sad that the reflection of the trees is interrupted by the grass of the field emerging through the flood. But there was no way around that problem and in this case something was better than nothing. I do at least like the way that the tops of the trees are held within the boundaries of the water, and I can console myself by saying that you don't always have to look for perfection to get something that, in its own terms, works.

Your ears should prick up when you find water in the place where you are out to take some photographs. Because water is one of the great allies of the photographer for the simple reason that it is so protean an element. As a still reflecting pool it can do everything the sky can do, but water goes on well beyond that: it can bend and colour light, it can enact its own drama in a wild sea, it can take on the astonishing appearance of molten metal, it can in a waterfall actually portray the passing of time in a stilled image – and so on. Always be alert to its moods and possibilities. It will always reward you.

112

RIVER THAMES AT WALLINGFORD, OXFORDSHIRE

Film: Ektachrome 64 ASA
Camera: 6 x 6 centimetres
Lens: Standard
Exposure: 1 second at f.22
Filters: None

POINTS TO WATCH

● *There is too much heavy black in the fore-ground. This picture would be better cropped above the fence. Try it with your hand and you will see how the main purpose of the photograph becomes much clearer.*

● *The ruffling of the water just where the reflections of the trees meet it is a little unsettling. Ideally that reflecting area should be quite still. Always wait for a lull in the breeze if you can.*

Water as Something Beautiful in Itself

RIVER CUCKMERE, SUSSEX

MOUSTIERS ST MAIRE, PROVENCE

Few sights are more beautiful than the still and reflecting light of a slow-moving river at dusk. The meanders of the Cuckmere in Sussex, rolling out to sea through a soft, round-edged valley in the Downs, provides a perfect image of ease and calm. The water is unruffled. The relative turbulence of the sky serves to heighten the smooth and balanced surface of the water. It would have been lovely if the river had picked up more light from the sky, but the one highlight on the right hand side does at least provide the low-key climax to an understated photograph: a gilded moment in a picture of shadows.

Here the water's reflection of the sky is better than the sky itself. The calm is absolute. It is an entirely unified picture in which everything is understood simply in different tones of pink.

This is water not as a reflective element but as a continuation of the landscape by other means. Here it is soft and inviting, the water becoming the most alluring of all places, a surface capable of the sort of miracles which grass and soil could never hope to match.

> Film: Fujichrome 50 ASA
> Camera: 6 x 6 centimetres
> Lens: Wide-angle
> Exposure: 1 second at f.22
> Filters: 81c warm-up

> Film: Ektachrome 64 ASA
> Camera: 6 x 6 centimetres
> Lens: Wide-angle
> Exposure: 1 second at f.22
> Filters: Low density grey graduated

POINTS TO WATCH

● *In a picture of calm one uncalm element can enhance rather than diminish the effect.*
● *Don't go home before the last drop of light has been squeezed from the sky. It is often at those marginal moments that something beautiful emerges from an everyday scene.*

POINTS TO WATCH

● *For this kind of effect an absolutely windless evening is vital. Everything must be sharp – no sentimentalised fuzziness here – and for everything to be sharp, the depth of field must be at its maximum. The aperture you use must therefore be small.*
● *With a small aperture you need a long exposure. Only a windless evening will give you an unblurred reed.*

The only time water is going to look truly wet and liquid is when it is backlit like this, seen as a bubbling, spilling surface, the eddied mass of a supremely mobile element caught at a literally unrepeatable moment. No picture of this could ever look exactly the same. This is one of the miraculous forms of water, a foundry swimming with molten metal, or at least a place in which the two elements of light and water are somehow fused. It is the opposite of the picture on the following page: not a single drop of light penetrates below this boiling surface.

Film: Fujichrome 50 ASA
Camera: 6 x 6 centimetres
Lens: Wide-angle
Exposure: 1/60 second at f.8
Filters: High density grey graduated

POINTS TO WATCH

● *To catch water fixed at a particular moment you must use quite a fast exposure, but to get a full depth of field the aperture must remain quite small. It is therefore necessary to have quite a fast film (at the expense of some graininess in the image) or restrict yourself to times of the the day when there is quite a lot of light.*

RIVER DORDOGNE, ARGENTAT, CORREZE

Aquamarine

CLIFFS AT TREEN, CORNWALL

Here is water not as a reflector, nor as a continuation of the landscape by other means, but as a transparent medium.
Of course, for water to be transparent to the light you must be relatively high above it, as I was here on the cliff top. And this was a wonderful evening. The white light that always comes creeping around the sides of a dark sky is reflected here off the pale underwater sand in a Cornish cove. The result is an extraordinary liquid green, water with the internal lights of a jewel. The slight ruffling from a breeze off the channel, the brilliant white of the surf, the theatrical low sidelighting in the last moment before sunset: if you think that these might be the conditions you will find, have no hesitation: drive straight to the nearest cliff, and if you are lucky you will find something like this, half-fjord, half-Bahama, water lit from within.

Film: Ektachrome 64 ASA
Camera: 6 x 6 centimetres
Lens: Wide-angle
Exposure: 1/8 second at f.16/f.22
Filters: Polarising, low density grey graduated

POINT TO WATCH

● *One apparently incidental element in the picture, the white rock in the foreground, is oddly enough the key to it. Block it out with your hand and the dark mass in the foreground kills the rest of the picture stone dead.*

Catching the Exact Moment

MARINA DI ALBARESE, TUSCANY

The sea was sweeping back and forth around this log on a beach near Pisa. The picture is pleasing because of the moment it was taken, the precise visual arrangement of parts within a highly mobile landscape. It would not have been successful if the sea had been up to the foreground because the smooth stability of the wood, planed down over many years by the workings of the sea, would not have been so pronounced and the sense of natural sculpture would have been lost. A large, frothy white surface in the foreground would have dominated the picture and the result would have been a mess. But at this moment, the waves have withdrawn from the beach, leaving it wet and reflective, and the log stands free of the water, a piece of giant flotsam on whose limbs the sunlight creates a rich amber warmth.

> Film: Fujichrome 100 ASA
> Camera: 6 x 6 centimetres
> Lens: Wide-angle
> Exposure: 1/60 second at f.11
> Filters: Polarising, low density grey graduated

POINTS TO WATCH

● *The picture would have been better without the small bridge of sand lying between the two parts of the tree. I tried to dig it away, but the sea always brought the sand back in.*
● *In order to balance the relatively sombre tones of the beach, I have used a grey-graduated filter.*

Buildings and the Landscape

Buildings can give a sense of proportion to a landscape; but the relationship between the two must be handled very carefully. This chapter points out the problems and the opportunities: how to set the building in the landscape, giving it its due and respecting the architect's intentions while avoiding the problems of distortion.

THERE IS A GREAT freedom about buildings in isolation: you can do almost what you like with them. This, for many years, has been one of my favourites. Not particularly because of the formal properties of the photograph (although if you take the thresher away with your hand, you will see that the picture dies without it, without its repetition of the four-part nature of the shed and its angle to the camera). No, what I like about this shed is the way it is like an old piece of landscape which has been made and remade, displaying its own half-sorry history.

Nothing is more readable in the landscape than the face of a building, and nothing more able to mimic the presence of a human being in it. Perhaps it is a little fanciful, but I always like to see this shed as a rather battered old man who is still trying to do his best in the worst of times. It is the way in which every conceivable material has been put to use with a thought only as to what it might do in the circumstances that makes this such an endearing shed. Nothing has been tarted up here. It is, in other words, an honest building. It is not pretending to be anything other than what it is and in that there is a real delight. That straightforwardness, an explicitness about oneself, is the pleasure of the close-up portrait of the human face. And in the landscape the only things that can come up with the same mixture of vanity, pride, experience and impending, half-arrested decay are the buildings scattered on its surface.

120

LA LANDE POURRIE, MANCHE

Film: Ektachrome 64 ASA
Camera: 6 x 6 centimetres
Lens: Wide-angle
Exposure: 1/4 second at f.22
Filters: 81b warm-up, low density grey graduated

POINTS TO WATCH

● *The vapour trail in the sky is annoying. I should have waited for it to clear but the light was going.*
● *The shadow is too deep on the right-hand side. But again there was no real choice; I had to expose for the building.*
● *I got here after a long traipse across a muddy field. I didn't have a ladder with me, but that would have improved the picture. From a higher standpoint the tops of the trees on the right would have come below the horizon.*

121

Placing the Structure in the Frame

TROO, LOIRE

You have to have a good look around a building. I arrived at the south side of this church and thought, 'No, I won't bother.' But I know from experience that first thoughts are usually hopeless, second worse, and that only third, fourth or fifth ever have anything to say for them. So I walked around the church, to the east end, up a little hill, and using my thumbs and index fingers as a makeshift frame, saw that this picture was there. I was right up against the churchyard fence and if it had been even one foot nearer the building I could not have got the picture. Because one thing above all is true when photographing buildings: you must never point your camera *up* at them, because to point a camera up is to make all the verticals – walls, drainpipes and so on – apparently converge. A building if treated in this way starts to look like a pyramid.

There is another point to look for here. Treat a building as you would a person's face. Fill the frame with a building and you will reveal its character. Look carefully for the creases and wrinkles.

> Film: Ektachrome 64 ASA
> Camera: 6 x 6 centimetres
> Lens: Wide-angle
> Exposure: 1/4 second at f.22
> Filter: Polarising

POINTS TO WATCH

● *Make sure that the bright patches on the walls retain the details of the stonework. Don't overexpose. Nothing looks worse than burnt-out, overbrightened areas.*
● *Pale stone buildings reflect their own light so the shadows will be of no great depth and will always be a little lighter than they look to the eye.*

LAVARDIN, NEAR VENDOME, LOIR-ET-CHER

Anything seen from below, looking up, takes on an air of importance. It dominates the picture rather than taking its place within it. The wall on the right and the shed on the left both frame the central tower and this too adds to its air of dominance. Conventionally, it is not considered right to put the main focus of interest in the middle. But here – as so often, in fact – it works, partly perhaps because the nicely designed baker's board at least half-draws one's attention to the side. In this way balance in pictures of buildings can be subtly achieved. And to make the balance subtle is often far more satisfactory than a more obvious symmetry which, because it can look so contrived, can remove the sense of reality from the picture. It all depends on what you are looking for: a sense of the real or a sense of something taken slightly away from the usual view of things. Here the effect is conversational, a village as you might see it.

Film: Ektachrome 64 ASA
Camera: 6 x 6 centimetres
Lens: Wide-angle
Exposure: 1/4 second at f.22
Filter: Polarising

POINT TO WATCH

● *This photograph has been cropped, taking away most of the foreground which, because the camera had to be kept level, contained far too much uninformative gravel.*

Actors on the Stage

NEAR GERARDMER, VOSGES

The little church and the tree-clump next to it make a single object. Together they share the centre of attention, with the grass field in front of them like an apron-stage stretching into the auditorium. It is a modest domestic scene between actors in the landscape, the buildings performing a perfect little drama of their own. Always look for this if you can, a complementary pair, a visual dialogue, a male-and-femaleness, a balance of opposites quietly conversing between themselves.

Film: Fujichrome 50 ASA
Camera: 6 x 6 centimetres
Lens: Short telephoto
Exposure: 1/2 second at f.32
Filter: 81b warm-up

POINT TO WATCH

● *The sky is too nondescript to have been left quite as naked as this. A graduated filter might have done it some good here, set at an angle so as not to invade the hillside and not too strong so that its presence would remain unnoticed.*

This is a picture made up up almost entirely of *suggestions* – the light on the wood at bottom right, the flickering light in the trees. The only element within it that makes a straightforward remark is the mill itself. But there is a family relationship between the colours and the quality of light in the different parts of the picture. In this family the building – as one solid block of colour, the sort of big splash which nature itself can almost never produce – anchors the composition. It becomes the base-plate around which the whole of the rest of the picture is built.

SOUTH OF RIAÑO, LÉON, SPAIN

Film: Fujichrome 50 ASA
Camera: 6 x 6 centimetres
Lens: Short telephoto
Exposure: 1/2 second at f.32
Filter: 81c warm-up

POINTS TO WATCH

● *A ladder and a higher viewpoint would have taken the trees out of the sky which would have improved coherence.*
● *No polarising filter was used here because to have done so would have taken the reflections out of the river and made the foreground too dark and in too much contrast to the rest of the picture.*

Burying a Building in a Landscape

NEAR CORTONA, TUSCANY

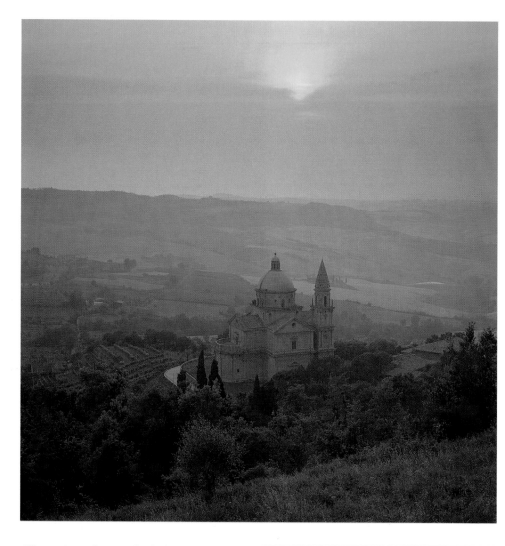

Sometimes there is the feeling that now, at this very moment, a building is showing itself off to its very best. I came across this Renaissance church near Cortona in the evening, at a time when every surface looks softened and absorbent, as if the watery light has leaked into every part of the picture; it seemed to be one such moment. Apart from the quality of the light, I think there is one key to this. And that is the way in which the building is buried in the landscape that surrounds it. It is not, as is usual, stood up against the sky, but included in the hills behind, so that the building is married and melded with the place it inhabits.

Film: Fujichrome 50 ASA
Camera: 6 x 6 centimetres
Lens: Short telephoto
Exposure: 1 second at f.32
Filters: 81c warm-up, low density grey graduated

POINT TO WATCH

● *It is always important to show the whole of a building, or at least enough for you to understand the way in which it works. I had to include the bottom of the apse wall and this meant including, unfortunately, the stretch of road which is the one element in the picture that does not share the dusky softness of texture of the rest of the landscape. This is a compromise and it prevents the picture from being quite perfect.*

I have never seen a place so suited to its name. The little millpond called the Miroir de Scey must have been named precisely because it had been seen in moments like this. Nothing in nature could be so still. So again I was lucky and I arrived at precisely the time I was supposed to arrive. It was an apparition. You can hardly see the join between the water and the hill behind it so that the mill looks as if it is suspended there. The background and foreground have become one. This is taking the principle of burying the building in its landscape almost as far as it can go. Here the mill hangs in its misty half-place as half-visibly, as a spider in its web. Look away and the building might disappear. Look again and it would have returned.

MIROIR DE SCEY, NEAR BESANÇON, DOUBS

Film: Fujichrome 50 ASA
Camera: 6 x 6 centimetres
Lens: Wide-angle
Exposure: 3 seconds at f.22
Filters: None

POINTS TO WATCH

● *The neon light in the building on the right should not be there. I waited for hours for the man to turn it off, but he never did.*

● *Fingers of greenery on the left and right make a mess and intrude on the image. A longer lens which would have cut them out would have cramped the building within the frame too much. Again, a compromise was necessary.*

● *The nature of mist is blue and here that blueness enhances the atmosphere. There would no point in using an ultraviolet or warm-up filter here.*

Making Something Strange

OLVERA, ANDALUCIA

The light coming from directly behind me slams straight on to the hilltop town. There is nothing mysterious or atmospheric about this light. It is the hard, bright, full-in-the-face light of midday. But isn't there something extraordinary and strange about this photograph? You might think that slash of white along the horizon is a natural phenomenon, an exposed stratum of white rock in the all-surrounding brown. Only a second glance reveals that it is a collection of individual buildings. So here the relationship of building to landscape has reached at least one form of paradoxical climax. Nothing could be more distinct than the difference between town and not-town, building and not-building in this picture. But at the same time that difference is so severe that the artificial has taken on the appearance of something natural. So do not think that you always have to make a building or collection of buildings in the landscape utterly straightforward. Always look for the strange

---

Film: Fujichrome 50 ASA
Camera: 6 x 6 centimetres
Lens: Telephoto
Exposure: 1/2 second at f.32/f.45
Filters: Polarising

POINT TO WATCH

● *The foreground, which is not as pretty as I would have liked it to be, could perhaps be cropped a little. But not entirely. The town needs a good spread of foreground to set it in its place and for once quantity matters here more than quality.*

The Big View

The big view is one of the most difficult of all landscapes to get right. It is too easy for a big landscape to look uninteresting unless you help the viewer's eye. The chapter describes some of these aids, leading you towards the distance, establishing a sense of scale and giving the picture a sense of narrative, of something happening.

THE MOUNTAINS of the Peloponnese, which have been seriously overgrazed, used to be covered in forest but now tend to look like bad skin. If one photographs them without any visual help, they can appear unapproachable and, because of that, uninteresting. One has to be led towards them and this visual path between the olives painted with fungicide takes the eye very easily and definitely in their direction.

Any avenue is good, simply for the obvious depth into the picture which it conveys. But for big views, they are almost invaluable.

This may sound like nannying, but avenues, like almost everything else, need very careful handling. You cannot imagine that you can slap down an avenue with some big and distant thing at the end of it, hope for the best and come up with a satisfying picture. Be patient with the composition, look very carefully at the things that go to make it up and then, as I had to here, make the picture work as well as you can.

Here, for example, I knew there was something wrong and the eye was not being led directly enough towards the distance. And then I realised: there were too many little white stones lying around on the soil in the foreground. I moved them, not wanting the distraction they would have involved, but I used a stick, standing to one side, poking and flicking away at them like some arcane fairground game. Nothing would have done more to ruin the picture than a series of large and obvious footprints in the foreground.

NORTH OF VYTINA, ARCADIA, GREECE

Film: Fujichrome 50 ASA
Camera: 6 x 6 centimetres
Lens: Wide-angle
Exposure: 1/8 second at f.16/f.22
Filters: Polarising, 81c warm-up, low density grey graduated

POINTS TO WATCH

● I have used the polarising filter to enrich the sky but this has had a cost. The reflected light off the olive tree leaves has been lost, leaving them looking flatter than they would otherwise have done.

● The warm-up filter has done well in enriching the red of the soil. This helps the picture structure, simply because the white trunks stand out against it so much more strongly.

Stepping Towards the Distance

Selassia, north of Sparta, Peloponnese, Greece

With a big view, it is the relationship between your own standpoint and the distant elements of the view which is all-important. Here you step in three giant strides towards the distant range, each step marked by something quite definite in itself: the trees and flowers; the church; and the grey snow-capped mountains. It isn't perfect. The trees have been damaged, the lower branches are dying, and the church has been over-restored so that it looks too pert, over-smartened when it should look relaxed and natural in the landscape. But the strength of the formal elements holds it all together despite this. This is in fact a picture which succeeds by leaving out the connections between its parts, loping off towards the horizon.

Film: Ektachrome 64 ASA
Camera: 6 x 6 centimetres
Lens: Wide-angle
Exposure: 1/2 second at f.22
Filter: Polarising

POINTS TO WATCH

● *Very important is the bright light on the church against the unlit background. Wait for the sun to play its tricks for you.*

● *The face of the church that is nearest to the camera is in shadow and the rest lit. This greatly enhances the three-dimensionality of an object.*

● *The picture might benefit from some cropping of the sky, to make more of the mountains and to avoid having the horizon coming halfway up the picture. Try it with your hand.*

LOCH STACK, SUTHERLAND

Here the small house is the fulcrum of the picture. It is the place you might want to get to. What lies beyond it is where you will then want to go on. In order to create this intelligible depth in the picture, the house can only be where it is, in the middle distance. Nearer would have made it too separate from the far hills; further away and it would have been too far from us as the viewer. A house plays this role so well because one automatically knows the size of windows and doors. They are scaled to human beings so they make their surroundings knowable by giving them a sense of proportion. A rock in the same place would not have worked.

Film: Ektachrome 64 ASA
Camera: 6 x 6 centimetres
Lens: Wide-angle
Exposure: 1/2 second at f.22
Filter: Polarising, fully polarised

POINTS TO WATCH

● *I should not have used the polarising filter. A glittery surface to the water would have been preferable and density of colour was not a priority here.*
● *The white face of the building makes the point better than if it had been painted a colour that was more in tune with the landscape. This is a case where the building has to stand out from the landscape in order to organise it.*

Giving a Looser Shape to the Landscape

POINTE DE SURGATTE, PYRENEES-ATLANTIQUES

The way in which the flock of sheep at the bottom mirrors the cloud at the back gives a shape to a mountain landscape that might otherwise have been difficult to orchestrate. The little building plays its familiar, fixing role, as the giver of scale and the still point in an otherwise very mobile scene. As it now stands, the organisation is just teetering on the edge of coherence, the elements in it as casual as a scarf draped across a shoulder.

Film: Ektachrome 64 ASA
Camera: 6 x 6 centimetres
Lens: Short telephoto
Exposure: 1/4 second at f.32
Filters: Polarising, low-density grey-graduated

POINT TO WATCH

● *The pink tinge to the cloud is produced by the graduated filter. The picture might have been better without it. Always try and avoid an effect which distracts from the main point.*

134

Rather than stepping back into the view, or having something like an avenue in the foreground that delivers the distant view for you, this road in the Welsh borders provides a sweet, curling line into the distance – a wiggle here, a bend there, passing the house, almost pausing at it, and then on over the brow to a destination one can only guess at. The distance is black with shadow, a sombre presence which alone prevents the picture from toppling over into sweetness. That massive background contains and, like the black sky in the picture of The Manger at Uffington (page. 108), disciplines the charming fore- and middle ground. In a way, the lane could be seen as a relaxed form of the avenue leading one towards the distance, an avenue that has loosened its belt and is wandering carelessly off into the distance.

Again, quite intuitively I have made the lane snake around the centre line of the picture, where it works as the picture's elastic spine.

> Film: Ektachrome 64 ASA
> Camera: 6 x 6 centimetres
> Lens: Wide-angle
> Exposure: 1/2 second at f.22
> Filter: Polarising

POINTS TO WATCH

● *The short telephoto lens compacts the scene, bringing the background into a closer relationship with the farmhouse.*
● *There is a subtle symmetry in the picture, with the lane snaking around its centre line and the blocks of field, wood and hill in understated balance.*

EGLWYSEG MOUNTAIN, CLWYD

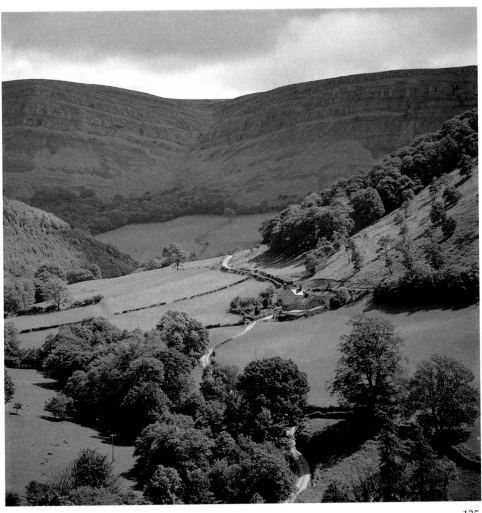

A Sense of Scale

ST BRIDE'S BAY, PEMBROKESHIRE

It is impossible to get any sense of scale in this picture unless you realise that the tiny blip of a figure on the edge of the water is a human being, fishing in the surf that is rolling in off the bay. That figure alone, a thing so out of scale with everything that surrounds him, reveals the bigness of the place and the size of the marine processes that are shaping it. Those rocks in the foreground are shorn off not in tiny, picked-at detail but at the scale of a city block. One lesson emerges: scale can be understood only in relative terms. Something big will only look big when set against something small.

Film: Ektachrome 64 ASA
Camera: 6 x 6 centimetres
Lens: Wide-angle
Exposure: 1/30 second at f.5.6
Filter: Medium density grey graduated

POINTS TO WATCH

● *The lighting conditions as ever are critical. Block out the far highlight on the sea to understand how important that is for the theatricality of the picture.*

● *I did not realise the importance of the figure when I was taking the picture. Allow the chance element to influence you whenever you can.*

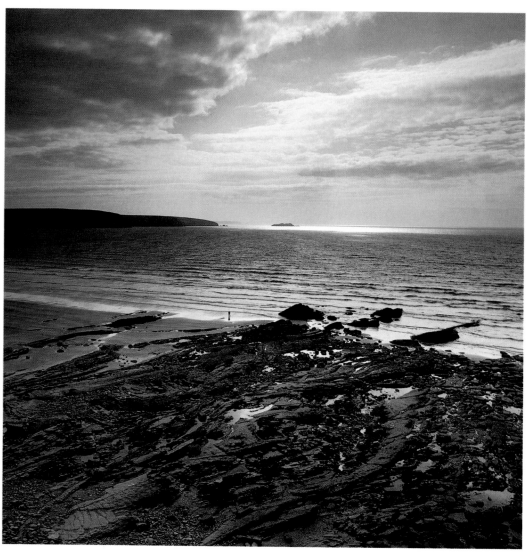

CLAGGAIN BAY, ISLAY, INNER HEBRIDES

I often wonder if this picture would have worked without the swan. Put your hand over it and the picture remains beautiful, doesn't it? The colour of the sea is so good, the pebbles of the beach are so cleanly and individually identified, the boarded ceiling of the sky is so fierce and dramatic and the pure bandedness of the composition is a pleasure in itself. So the single swan is not essential to the picture. But it does do something: it pins the place to the spot and for that, at least, any photographer is going to be grateful. And it provides the element of the unexpected: the grace of a swan in such a visually harsh and northern scene plays the part of a mole on the cheek of a beauty.

Film: Fujichrome 50 ASA
Camera: 6 x 6 centimetres
Lens: Wide-angle
Exposure: 1/4 second at f.22
Filter: High density grey graduated

POINTS TO WATCH

● *It is important in this picture to have the immediate foreground as sharp as a knife. Press the shutter at the stillest possible moment. And for that it's worth waiting.*

● *Be very careful indeed when using a heavy graduated filter like this. If it begins to look like a filter rather than a natural sky, then the effect it is producing is too strong. To my eye, this looks as if it is just on the edge of being too much.*

The Intimacies of the Landscape

The detail always represents a new way of looking. Whether isolating a graphic pattern, highlighting the corner of a village that seems to sum it all up or suddenly noticing an aspect of nature which the eye normally slides over, the detail is often the approach that reveals the essential qualities of a place.

A SINGLE ROCK masquerades as a lump of abandoned bullion. I had seen it as I was walking along the shore and when still a long way away. It looked almost like a traffic light in its monotone surroundings. But, coming closer, the eye goes on to meet far more in a place than it can first recognise. This became as strange and mystery-laden a landscape as you could find. With its broken and eaten leaves, mixed with flakes of seaweed, the abandoned detritus of an estuary shore, the water boatman resting on the stone, the solid rock surrounded by decay – it is, for me, almost like looking inside a magician's box. Less, like this, can be more: no giant views, no famous landmarks, but the whole workings of a landscape clustered around a golden stone.

It is always important when photographing a detail to make sure that you hold the picture at the right level. To have isolated this stone from its immediate surroundings would have stripped it of much of its meaning. The rock illuminates its own miniature landscape. Without it, the old scurf of dropped leaves would have meant very little indeed, no more than the rubbish in the bottom of the puddle. But it is equally true that the rock itself, shorn of its surroundings, would have lost too, and would have taken on the air of strangeness which, for example, the trunk of the plane tree on page 145 has. Even at this scale, the relationship between the wider landscape and the most prominent object in it is all-important.

ISLE OF SKYE, INNER HEBRIDES

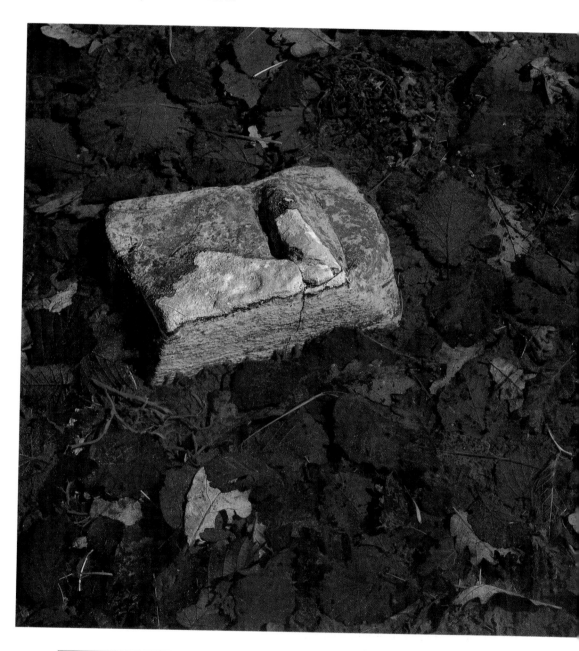

Film: Ektachrome 64 ASA
Camera: 6 x 6 centimetres
Lens: Wide-angle
Exposure: 1 second at f.22
Filter: Polarising, fully polarised

POINTS TO WATCH

● *Make sure there is nothing like a milk bottle top or any other distracting rubbish in a picture like this.*

● *If you think the photograph would look better with the rock wettened and glisteny, then have no hesitation in splashing water all over it. The leaves around the stone might also have been rearranged with some improvement. Perhaps there might have been a few more pale green leaves in there to add extra highlights.*

Close Attention

ARQUES, NEAR LIMOUX, PROVENCE

LE CASTELLET, PROVENCE

Film: Fujichrome 50 ASA
Camera: 6 x 6 centimetres
Lens: Short telephoto
Exposure: 1/4 second at f.22/f.32
Filters: None

Film: Ektachrome 64 ASA
Camera: 6 x 6 centimetres
Lens: Wide-angle
Exposure: 1 second at f.22
Filters: Polarising, 81b warm-up

Quite often, when you are out taking photographs, you find that the impact of a particular part of the scene in front of you will be more than the whole. The building of which the above picture is a part was, as a whole, muddled by telegraph wires and all sorts of other distractions. But the detail is clean, allowing you to look hard at the colours and textures of the thing in front of you. It also allows something that is simply interesting in itself – a pot or some roses or even a pair of hinges – to take on a role far beyond the part it plays in real life. Photographs of details can in this way be a sort of fantasy zone, miniature landscapes in which very small things take on the importance and place which might be taken by a building or even a mountain in the width of the landscape as a whole. But there is something else in a detailed study: a sense of the preciousness of things, of giving something, for once, the sort of attention which is usually given only in the process of making or preserving or training it. In this way taking photographs of details can feel almost literally creative and you will find yourself absorbed for hours arranging and rearranging the miniature landscapes which detailed photography involves

POINT TO WATCH

● *Details always work well if the light is coming from the side. The slightest bumps or hollows will then create shaping shadows.*

POINT TO WATCH

● *I used a polariser here to knock off the reflections in the shadow. Details require extra close attention – no imbalance, no contamination. I cleaned the cigarette ends out of here. There are unfortunately some tiny bits of paper left. I also experimented with the shutters. When I had both of them open, it took attention away from the urn. With both closed it looked uninviting and cold. This position seemed the most balanced.*

A little house in the Loire valley, slightly the worse for wear and with the paint on the shutters needing another coat (but what a French colour that peeling, fading blue-grey is!): a classic example of the way in which a tightly controlled and isolated detail can describe the whole world of which it is a part. Here is the French village. It takes no imagination to see the people who live in this house, their clothes, the way they stand and greet each other, their bikes, their food, their pets, their clothes...

NEAR ORLÉANS, LOIRE VALLEY

POINT TO WATCH

● *The polariser brings out the reds and blackens the windows. Extreme colour contrast in a small compass always works well. Grey shutters, tan walls, the red swag of roses and the black of the windows: this is the kind of combination to look for.*

Film: Ektachrome 64 ASA
Camera: 6 x 6 centimetres
Lens: Short telephoto
Exposure: 1/2 second at f.32
Filter: Polarising

A Pleasing Pattern

NEAR TARBERT, ISLE OF HARRIS, OUTER HEBRIDES

A peat bog in the Outer Hebrides can be the very ugliest of landscapes, without shape or form, the colours dull, the look little more than a pudding that has been left out in the rain. I was about to leave when from a chink in the corner of my eye I saw this. I saw the repeated angle of the water plants – like a *corps de ballet* – the velvety water, the vibrant yellow set against the black. All those might have been there in a wider picture, but diluted. And this is the point: the detail concentrates the flavours. To make it small means to make it strong, a dense essence of landscape, as distilled as whisky, a sip of landscape concentrate.

Film: Fujichrome 50 ASA
Camera: 6 x 6 centimetres
Lens: Standard
Exposure: 1/4 second at f.22
Filter: Polarising, fully polarised

POINT TO WATCH

● *There is really only one point to watch: make it whole, exclude the excludable and think only of the pattern, not of the place. You must not try and be fair to the landscape. That is not the point. Ruthless excision of the boring can be the only principle. Think of the picture frame as a stage on which you are arranging the players. What happens outside is irrelevant.*

The trees in this bit of Spanish landscape had been burnt. The only impact of this picture comes from the completeness with which the pattern covers the picture surface. If you are relying on recurring elements in a detail then those elements must recur across the whole length and breadth of the image. Imagine for a moment the burnt trees and the flowers petering out at the the bottom left hand corner. The whole picture falls apart and becomes nothing more than a patch of rough ground, not, as it is here, a perfect square cut from a natural tapestry.

GUADALUPE, CACERES, SPAIN

Film: Agfachrome 1000 ASA
Camera: 6 x 6 centimetres
Lens: Short telephoto
Exposure: 1/4 second at f.32
Filters: None

POINT TO WATCH

● *This picture was taken on a fast film and as a result is rather grainy. But to treat something so finely worked in this rough way is often a good idea, a visual contraction in terms which adds a sense of energy that would have been absent in a more finely polished picture.*

Strange Realities

BACINO ORSEOLE, VENICE

Film: Fujichrome 50 ASA
Camera: 6 x 6 centimetres
Lens: Standard
Exposure: 1/8 second at f.22
Filters: None

POINT TO WATCH

● *Keep something at least of the gondola prow recognisable in the photograph. With broken reflections in water choose a moment of relative calm. This frame is only one of many I made, never quite sure at the time which one was going to work. This is an occasion where I would recommend exposing quite a large number of frames.*

Remove something from its surroundings and in some ways you are removing it from reality. These images are at first difficult to piece into the real world. Neither of them has been filtered or distorted in any way. The bark of a plain tree in Le Tholonet or the reflection of a pair of gondola prows in a Venetian canal do appear like this to the human eye but are never seen. The whole secret of finding this sort of photograph lies in actually looking at something over which the eye might normally slide. And to achieve this the only possible advice is: be vigilant and make your eye a lens.

LE THOLONET, BOUCHES-DU-RHONE

Film: Ektachrome 64 ASA
Camera: 6 x 6 centimetres
Lens: Wide-angle
Exposure: 1 second at f.22
Filters: None

POINT TO WATCH

● *It is important even in this miniature scene to get as great a depth of field as possible. Use a very small aperture and long exposure. With something strange, you must allow the viewer to see as much of it as you can. The fact that the right-hand edge of the tree trunk is visible helps a great deal in identifying the subject.*

The Final Shape

After you have exposed your frames and had them returned from the processors you must decide what shape prints you would like to make of them. Ideally, the picture was already perfectly composed in the viewfinder of the camera, but that cannot always be the case. The chapter shows you how to improve your pictures by cropping them.

I WALKED OUT IN armpit-high fisherman's waders to reach this point midstream of a cold and fast-running river, thick with melt-water from the snows in the Pyrenees. I knew when I arrived in the valley, with this wonderful sky, bannered with cloud, that there was a good picture here.

I exposed some frames from the bank but they did not work and so I found myself strapping on the waders. The picture I found in midstream works on the basis of a system of interlocking symmetries. The first is hinged to the apex of the rock in midstream, creating a star-shape over the whole frame. The two banks of the river come away and down from that point; the horizon of the ridge on the left and the tops of the trees on the right move away and up

from that point. The texture of the two areas they enclose – the flecked sky and the broken water of the river – are reflections of each other.

Within this radial system of symmetries, there is another three-banded element consisting of the low boulders in the foreground, the central boulder and the distant mountain, three steps back into a landscape of perfectly arranged parts.

You couldn't cut anything out of this picture without diminishing it. All the cropping was done on the spot with the frame of the camera itself. And I knew it at the time, a whooping sense of delight. This was indeed the final shape there in front of me, when for a moment the landscape itself was displaying all the brilliance of a flag.

146

RIVER ESERA, SOUTH OF CAMPO, HUESCA

Film: Fujichrome 50 ASA
Camera: 6 x 6 centimetres
Lens: Wide-angle
Exposure: 1/8th second at f.16
Filters: Polarising, 81a warm-up

POINTS TO WATCH

● *This is a case where the polarising filter comes into its own, accentuating the drama of the sky.*
● *If I had panned too far to the left there would have been too much unlit hill. Reduce very dark areas as much as you can.*

● *In the light of the setting sun, the last twenty minutes seem to go by in a flash. A few minutes later there would have been no light in the left of the picture, the bushes on the island on the left would have been unlit and there would have been no picture here to have been taken.*
● *A higher vantage point is always better than a lower one and if I had dared I would certainly have tried to have taken my stepladder out into the middle of the stream. But I did not think the collapse and drowning of photographer and camera was quite worth it.*

Cutting out the Competition

AIOZ, NAVARRA

As this picture stands, there is too much of the track in the foreground. It competes with that astonishing cloud for its place in the picture. It is quite clear that the giant ball of a cloud is the more interesting of the two. Put your hand over the cloud look at the picture again. It works perfectly well, becoming a photograph of what you expect of the Spanish plains: a gritty road disappearing into nowhere, long long horizons, a place of almost shadeless heat. But then take your hand away and the picture returns to its state of imbalance, of indecisiveness.

One has to go and it is obviously the track or most of it. It has been cropped to this effect on the opposite page. It becomes a photograph of something else entirely. The minute scale of things on the landscape are revealed if one cloud can so dominate such a wide sliver of terrain. The cloud is an object of huge and fuzzy drama. The photograph has started to assume the air of a picture of earth's atmosphere taken from space.

But things have changed in the landscape as well. The clump of trees on the knoll in the distance has become important for the way the picture works: without them there is no focal point, with them the scale of the cloud is revealed, or to be more precise the difference in the scale of things in the landscape and in the atmosphere is revealed. It has become a picture of how the global meets the local.

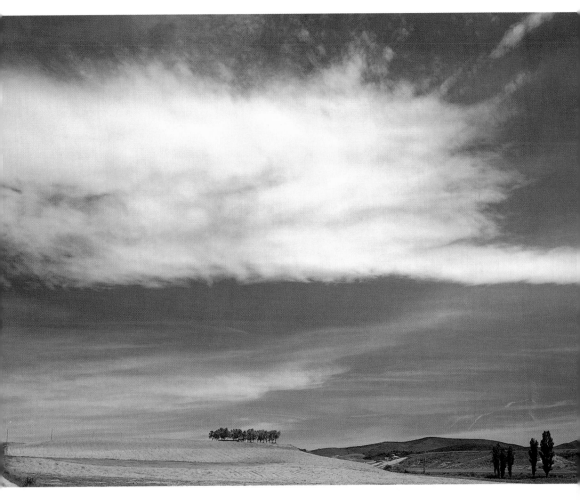

Film: Fujichrome 50 ASA
Camera: 6 x 6 centimetres
Lens: Wide-angle
Exposure: 1/4 second at f.22
Filters: 81c warm-up

POINTS TO WATCH

● The way in which the left-hand edge of the track is clipped off by the frame is annoying and careless. It would also have been better if the right hand edge of the track came down to meet the bottom right hand corner of the frame. One of these faults was avoidable – it is sheer carelessness – the other is something which might have been wished for in a perfect world. Nevertheless, it may well be precisely these failures of minute detail which make the bottom half of the original picture slightly unsatisfying. Imagine the full square frame with the stub end of the track broadening out to occupy the whole of the foot of the picture. Would the urge to crop it still have been there in that case?

● I wonder, looking at it now, whether the crop has been made a little too high. Would the cropped picture have been more satsfying if the little sliver of yellow had extended right to the edge of the frame under the five poplar trees? I think it might well have been, somehow completing the movement of the landscape itself from left to right across the picture. As it stands, the field looks a little truncated, and that is an impression which one should try never to give. Attempt always to make the meaning of a picture whole.

● It would have been much nicer if the cloud had been complete and not cut into on the left hand side. But this was a compromise. I needed the balance in the landscape between the track on the left and the little group of poplars on the right. If I had moved the track any nearer the centre of the frame, that balance would have been disturbed, the crucial group of trees in the centre on the horizon would have been moved out of position and the whole composition of the picture would have fallen apart.

Cleaning Up

EAST OF RONDA, MALAGA, SPAIN

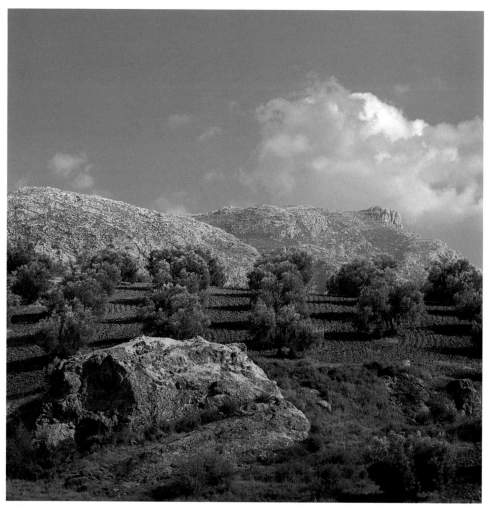

The lines of olives in the background are a pattern which I would have liked to make much clearer in the photograph. As it is, I did not really succeed. The trees fall out of the picture to left and right and the structure of the landscape is muddled.

The rock in the foreground is of huge importance in the way the picture works, but it is not in the right place. The scurfy patch at bottom right is a classic instance of what not to include in a photograph, a jumbly, uninformative area of dead ground, into which the meaning of the picture leaks away. It is, in itself, a sign of loss of control.

So here it is a question of salvaging what I can from the picture to make it something

that pleases. What can one do? First of all we have to lose the sky because it is weak, a wretched little sky, which shows all the signs of impatience, neither balanced, nor shapely in itself, nor reflecting the forms of the landscape beneath it. The bottom right of the picture has to follow it and the great crusted rock in the foreground has to be brought on to centre stage. This is a simple process of cleaning up in which you can be as ruthless as you like.

The cropped result, opposite, at least has a certain look of integrity to it. The boulder becomes twinned to the mass of raw limestone mountain in the background. The olives, although still not as coherent as I would like them (there is for example the area at the back on the left which is a little tentative and undecided) are now more plainly ranked than before. The asymmetries of the sky have been removed and it now forms a fairly harmless band at the top of the picture, undistracting, the fourth stripe against which the banding of the landscape itself is set. Tidier, not perfect, but a perfectly workable picture.

there is no sky to speak of you can always take it out. No sky will always be better than a poor sky.
● *Cropping like this can salvage something, but you can be sure that it can rarely do as well as patience and skill when you are out in the landscape itself. Try not to trust to cropping to make your pictures work for you. Look hard and be patient when the camera is in your hand.*

POINTS TO WATCH

● *I should perhaps have waited for a better sky. If some beautiful clouds had appeared I wouldn't have taken the sky out of the picture. But where*

Film: Fujichrome 50 ASA
Camera: 6 x 6 centimetres
Lens: Standard
Exposure: 1/4 seconds at f.22
Filter: Polarising

The Photograph Designed for Cropping

SOUTH OF ANDUJAR, JAEN, SPAIN

Incredibly strong blocks of colour and almost rigid geometries like these are the moments when the natural world starts to take on its most unnatural aspect. Here is a landscape which a child might draw but which, you might think, could never occur in the subtle setting of the real world. But it does and when you are faced with a picture like this, the natural inclination is to treat the landscape in the way that, in a sense, it is treating itself. Exaggerate it, take the signs it is making and push them as far as you can go. Of course with colours and sunshine like this you must use a polarising filter, saturating the film with colour so rich that it is almost stark.

And then when you have the colour oozing out of the film you must decide on what shape the photograph must have to bring out this intense unnaturalness. Cropping can be – and often is – a very disrespectful process. It is not about showing the full reality of what is there. The very opposite of that. It is taking the landscape and shearing away anything that might get in the way of a particular meaning you want to convey.

When I was taking this picture, I knew I would have no need of the sky when it came to printing it. The sky would set the olives and poppies too sweetly in their real setting. I didn't want such clear information. I wanted to mystify and amaze with the picture. This is something I almost never do.

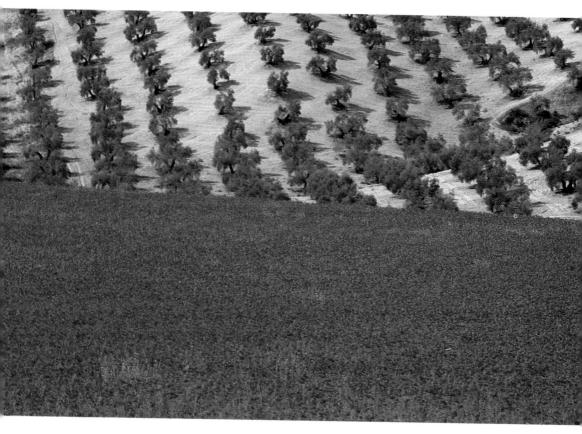

I am usually keen on explanation, clarity and fullness of meaning. But here I was doing no more than respond to the landscape on its own terms: treating coarsely something that was almost almost unbelievably coarse itself. The cropping had to take out all the sky, all hint of a horizon and and those patches in the field of poppies where the density of colour was not quite all it might have been.

You will hear many photographers say that cropping is a vulgar and lazy practice. Everyone should compose their pictures in the viewfinder or on the ground-glass screen of the camera. It is, like all counsels of perfection, a very seductive and tempting idea. No doctoring after the fact, no fiddling for effect where you had failed in front of the landscape itself, no 'cheating.' And part of me is very sympathetic to that. I love the idea of photography as a pure art, a straightforward response to landscape of man with a camera in his hand. But I know too that it is not always like that. I know there are days when things do not go sweetly, that the world is not falling in to your lap. Of course it doesn't! And of course not all photographs will work as they were framed up. One can look at cropping as an improving art, one that can be practised with delicacy and skill. It will always be useful in the making of a point, in highlighting a particular aspect of a photograph which would have been lost without any cropping. I must say that the pictures I have taken which continue to please me were all composed in the camera itself. But perhaps there is no need to be quite so pious about it. They are, after all, only photographs.

Film: Fujichrome 50 ASA
Camera: 6 x 6 centimetres
Lens: Telephoto
Exposure: 1 second at f.45
Filters: Polarising

POINT TO WATCH

● *Looking at the cropped picture now, I wonder if the sky should have been removed. Would a three banded flag of a picture have done the job better than this two banded slice? I am not sure. And again it is worth considereing whether the division between the poppies and olives is quite right. Should the line between them be slightly lower down the picture?*

Glossary

Aperture The hole in the **diaphragm** through which light enters the camera to fall on the film. Varying apertures control **exposure**.

ASA The abbreviation for **A**merican **S**tandards **A**ssociation used to measure **film speed**. Films that are very sensitive to light, or fast films, have a high ASA number and those which need a longer exposure have a low ASA number.

Backlighting A situation where the main source of light is behind the subject of the photograph and so the light falls directly on the lens. Often a beautiful form of lighting, giving a halo to the subject, but in these circumstances you must watch for **flare**.

Bracketing Used particularly with transparency film as a way of not losing opportunities, a system of making exposures above and below what you guess to be the right one but are not quite sure.

Colour conversion filter A filter used to re-adjust a film to lighting conditions for which it was not manufactured, for example an 80a, which is blue, must be used when daylight-balanced film is used under tungsten light and an 85b when tungsten-balanced film is used in daylight.

Colour correction filter Another term for **warm-up filter**.

Contrast The difference between the darkest and lightest parts of a photograph. Make it a point of principle never to have the lightest parts so light nor the darkest so dark that no detail is visible in them.

Definition The precision with which the photograph has reproduced the subject. High **film speed**, shallow **depth of field**, failure to focus the camera or to make the tripod rigidly still all reduce definition.

Density The darkness or paleness of a photograph. As a rule, slow **film speeds** will increase colour saturation and so the density of a photograph.

Depth of Field A measure of the distance between the furthest and the nearest object in the photograph which are both in focus. Small **apertures** increase depth of field, large ones reduce it.

Diaphragm The mechanism in the lens consisting of a circle of metal blades that control the size of the **aperture.**

Emulsion The light-sensitive coating on a film on which the photographic image is recorded.

Exposure The amount of light falling on the film which is controlled by a combination of the **aperture** and the length of time the shutter is open.

f-number The measure of the aperture. A large f-number means a small aperture, a small f-number means a large aperture.

Film speed The sensitivity of a film to light. High-speed films are useful for freezing rapid motion in a subject, for using in low-light conditions and for making a photograph with a large **grain**. Low-speed films achieve a far greater colour-saturation and achieve richer colour-effects in a landscape.

154

Filter A glass or plastic sheet placed over the front of the lens to alter the quality of the light entering it. Several different sorts of filter can be used at one time.

Flare When strong light, from the sun or a lamp, shines directly into the camera, it can bounce off elements within the lens and create bright, geometrically shaped, over-exposed areas on the image. This is flare and can often be avoided by using a **lens-hood**.

Grain The large particles that appear on an image either when it is greatly enlarged or when a very fast film has been used.

Graduated filter A series of filters, coming in a variety of different densities, from low to high, and colours, including grey, tobacco, blue and so on. The filters darken only one part of the photograph. They are consistently useful in bringing the sky within the same exposure range as the landscape below it, although they must be used carefully when the horizon is interrupted by trees, hills, buildings and so on: nothing looks worse than half a hill bright and half artificially darkened.

Lens hood A cloth hood that fits on to the front of the lens to shade it from direct light and so avoid **flare**. With a wide-angle lens be careful not to catch part of the hood in the corner of the photograph. A hand can sometimes do just as well.

Neutral density filter A colourless grey filter that cuts down the amount of light reaching the film over the whole surface of the photograph. Particularly useful with long exposures where you want to record the movement of the subject in front of the lens without overexposing the film.

Polarising filter A filter that cuts out the polarised light which is usually created by reflections off a surface. It has the effect of enriching colour in both the sky and the landscape.

Shutter speed The length of time the film remains exposed.

Standard lens The lens that represents without distortion or compression a view of a landscape similar to the unaided eye.

Stop The unit by which an exposure is measured. A change of one stop, either in **shutter speed** or in **aperture**, represents a doubling or halving of the amount of light reaching the film.

Telephoto lens A lens that apparently brings the subject closer to the camera. It compresses elements within a landscape and has a shallow **depth of field**.

Tungsten balance film Film that has been adjusted to read the correct colours of a subject when lit by the artificial light created by an incandescent tungsten filament.

Ultra-violet radiation Part of the spectrum of light emitted by the sun which is invisible to the human eye but can be picked up by colour film as a bluish cast. An ultra-violet filter should be used to cut this out, particularly in hot, dry climates.

Warm-up filter Another name for the 81 series of **colour-correction filters**, used to add warmth and knock the blue coldness out of photographs, particularly in the shade.

Wide-angle lens A lens that encompasses a wider slice of the landscape than a standard lens.

Technical Notes

Camera

Every photograph in this book was taken with a Hasselblad 6 x 6 centimetres roll-film camera. I should explain why this is the perfect choice for me. First, the size of the transparency, which is about four times the area of a 35 mm transparency, means that the quality and texture of the final print will never suffer from enlargement. Secondly, the roll film is loaded into a removable chamber at the back of the camera and so it is possible to change films (black and white to colour transparency, fast to slow, slide film to polaroid for a near-instant check on exposure levels) without wasting frames on each film. And thirdly, the camera is heavy, bulky and unautomated. That might seem to be a disadvantage but I have found this to be exactly the right equipment for the sort of photographs I like to take. With a camera like this you always have to spend some time with the landscape, preparing yourself and the camera, and that time is never wasted.

Tripod

Almost nothing is more important than the reliability and strength of your tripod. Photographs that need good definition right up to the immediate foreground need long exposures and complete stability for the camera. Get as heavy a tripod as you think you can carry. It is also well worthwhile buying a tripod that includes a spirit-level, which is a far more trustworthy guide to a level horizon than your own eye.

Light meter

Many modern cameras include a through-the-lens light meter which, together with the automatic exposure controls, adjusts the settings for you. This is all right for a beginner but I would always recommend moving beyond that to a hand-held spot-meter with which, like one lens of a pair of binoculars, you can measure the intensity of light in any part of the photograph. That inevitably brings you closer involvement with the light conditions that surround you.

Film

Most of the photographs in this book have been taken on rather slow colour transparency film, either Ektachrome 64 ASA or Fujichrome 50 ASA. There is no doubt that this sort of film needs quite precise control and for any one photograph reproduced here I probably made four or five different exposures, precisely because with this sort of film very little adjustment can be made later at the processing stage. Colour negative film and black and white film are both far more generous to the photographer who has made incorrect exposures, which can be adjusted for in the processing and printing stages. So why choose colour transparency film? Because only it can convey in sharp detail the true colour, richness and beauty of the landscape. And that, of course, in the end, is what I am there for.

Index